Voices *that* Carry

*Conversations With Some Of
The Evangelical Church's Most
Interesting And Influential People*

BY WARREN SMITH

Copyright © 2005 by Warren Smith.

Voices That Carry
Edited by Warren Smith

Printed in the United States of America

ISBN # 1-59781-694-9

All rights reserved solely by the author. The author guarantees all contents are original and do not infringe upon the legal rights of any other person or work. No part of this book may be reproduced in any form without the permission of the author. The views expressed in this book are not necessarily those of the publisher.

Unless otherwise indicated, Bible quotations are taken from the New International Version. Copyright © 1973, 1978, 1984 International Bible Society.

www.xulonpress.com

Table of Contents

Acknowledgments 4

Introduction 5

In The Arena
Gary Bauer 9
Ken Connor 19
Tom Minnery 27
John Paulk 34
Mark Sanford 42
Jim Towey 49

Academics, Pastors, and Theologians
Norman Geisler 54
Haddon Robinson 63
Stanley Hauerwas 74
Jim White 84

Media and the Arts
Joel Belz 93
Marvin Olasky 101
Nichole Nordeman 111
Michael Card 121
Robert Whitlow 131
Lauren Winner 140

Appendix 152

Index 153

Acknowledgements

This book would not have come about without the cooperation of all the men and women interviewed herein. For their willingness to submit to my questions, I am grateful.

I am also grateful to Kim Pickering. As the art director for World Newspaper Publishing, she was responsible for the production of this book. But her contributions to this project go far beyond graphics and production. A writer and editor in her own right, she truly helped shape this book and the individual interviews. Her contributions were indispensable. When Kim left our company to become a full-time mother, Bethel Dirks took over this project and saw it to completion.

Finally, I would like to thank my wife Missy. Many of these interviews were conducted on evenings, weekends, or as part of long trips away from home. Such focus and clarity as I was able to maintain during these interviews is due to her efforts at holding down the home front.

Introduction

There is something special about the human voice. That specialness derives in part from its particularity, its specificity. The importance and power of this granular particularity is something every journalism student learns in his first reporting class. "Specificity is the soul of credibility" is, or should be, one of the first principles an aspiring journalist learns. I'll never forget, as a student journalist, writing, "Many people believe...". My teacher handed the story back to me with this remark in the margin: "If many people believe it, it should be easy to find one and quote him here."

As it turned out, it wasn't so easy. In some cases, in fact, it wasn't possible at all. Maybe there weren't so many who believed, or thought, or felt what I thought they did. Maybe I should be a better listener, and ask better questions, if I wanted to be a better writer. For even then I had in mind that being a better writer meant being a more convincing, more truthful writer.

Indeed, if the goal of journalism is to "tell the truth," as I believe it is, then achieving this granular particularity, this specificity, is essential. Most journalism today lacks that soul of credibility precisely because it does not capture this gritty specificity. It generalizes, it assumes. It fails to do the hard work of reporting, of listening and accurately recording what is said.

This is especially true when it comes to the mainstream media's portrayal of Christians. In this regard, there seems to be two trends. On the one hand, we often see mainstream reporters letting the most freakish and grotesque represent all of Christendom. A recent BBC World Service report on the state of religion in America, for example, began at a "cowboy church" in Nashville and ended at a "Bibleland" exhibit in Orlando, stopping in Dayton,

Tennessee, to talk about the Scopes Monkey Trial.

The other trend is to assume there is a monolithic "religious right" choir, singing in unison to the drumbeat of leaders who strike up the band when it comes time to make noise about abortion, homosexuality, gambling, or pornography. These journalists portray us always as "against," never "for." We're "anti-choice," never "pro-life." We're "anti-gay" (or worse). Always in opposition, always reactionary.

It is true that in a world tending toward disorder, the reactionary position is often the right position. But we Christians should not be cowed by this accusation that we are constantly reactionary. For even this conclusion – that Christians are opposed to disorder and chaos – presupposes an understanding of, or at least an inkling of, an orderly world. A beautiful vision of a loving God and careful creator. That this vision might be the true motivation of Christian activists is rarely considered by those in the mainstream media.

But there are those who know that a fully developed biblical worldview recognizes that "the earth is the Lord's, and the fullness thereof," and that a religious sensibility, a biblical worldview, can and should inform all areas of life. There are people out there who know that and are struggling to bring that perspective to all of life, and attempting to give this struggle a voice. These are the people, these are the voices, in this book.

Of course, a full and complete biblical worldview does not present itself at once. That should be obvious to anyone who has read the Bible itself. God tells Adam, in the Garden of Eden, to "name the animals." God brings each animal to Adam, who in his pre-lapsarian state in close communion with God, sees the very nature of the animal, and the name Adam gives the animal reflects that insight and understanding. Later, at the Tower of Babel, God's judgment on mankind is to scatter languages. What we call things no longer has that intimate relationship to the thing itself. We now have different words for the same thing. What is the true nature of things? Can the words we know ever capture that "true truth"?

Well, maybe. For God does not allow us to give up on words. We Christians are people of the Word. Scripture, of course, but also the "Word made flesh." Jesus comes among us and tells us stories.

Indeed, scripture employs the strategy of the good journalist throughout. When the Pharisees questioned the blind man who Jesus healed, he had a simple response: "I once was blind, but now I see." It was a simple declaration from an unlettered man, but it confounded the lawyers and religionists of his day. The Apostle John, on the island of Patmos, writes the entire book of Revelation in obedience to a single command: "Write down what you see."

The faithful recording of the words of credible witnesses: that's what good journalism, and good theology, are all about. It is my prayer that it is what this book is all about, too.

Warren Smith
Charlotte, NC
July 2005

In The Arena

Salt & Light

GARY BAUER

Perhaps no pro-family Christian activist has done more to take their religious beliefs into the public square in recent years than Gary Bauer. After serving for eight years in the Reagan administration, he took the Family Research Council (FRC) to national prominence. He resigned as president of the FRC to run for president, participating in a half-dozen national debates and generally elevating discussion of issues related to abortion and other important issues. This interview took place in 2003 when Bauer was in North Carolina to speak to more than 1,000 people at the annual fundraising banquet for Room At The Inn, a Catholic-sponsored home for unwed mothers.

Warren Smith: A lot of ink has been spilled about what has changed in the country since September 11. I have been wondering whether some of the positive changes will be permanent. My fear is that the negative changes – restrictions on liberty – might be permanent and some of the positive changes – such as a heightened awareness of the blessings we enjoy – might be temporary. What are your thoughts?

Gary Bauer: The jury is out on whether or not the changes are permanent or not, but one of the most obvious things is that up until September 10 we were talking about cutting the defense budget. Even the Bush administration put a proposal on the table to legalize eight-million illegal immigrants in the country. There were a lot of things going on with both parties that I think reflected a certain softness in thinking about the world and the challenges we face. Now, I think those kinds of ideas are on the back burner for a long time and are not going to be brought up for a very long time.

In the last ten to twelve years we have horrible cut backs on defense and intelligence gathering. We have allowed the borders of the United States to be treated as if they didn't exist. Those things seem to be changing.

The tougher question is whether we are in the midst of a spiritual renewal because of September 11. I hope we are, because that will make a lot more difference in the future of the country than even some of the other important things I mentioned. There are some signs we are in some sort of a renewal. I have a friend who says that even in secular, liberal New York, if you walk around at night, you are almost never out of earshot from someone singing "God Bless America," which is a pretty amazing thing for New York City. A lot of kids are praying in schools, whether the ACLU likes it or not. There seems to be more of a willingness to publicly express religious faith. We'll see if it continues. I hope it will.

WS: But you don't sound convinced that we are in the middle of a spiritual renewal.

GB: Well, it's hard to know. The last 30 years of America has been period of cultural decline and there is still an amazing hostility in some quarters to religion. In fact, Americans seem to have taken the lesson of September 11 [to be] that [since] radical Muslims cite their faith, this is proof that faith should never be a motivator in public life. I think [that] is bizarre lessons to get out of all this. I do think the jury is out. I am optimistic that the country is turning back to God, but we will have to wait and see.

WS: On the morning of September 11 you were in your car. Did you literally see the plane go into the Pentagon?

GB: Yes. I was heading into Washington to take part in a press conference on the issue of Sudan, where there is a radical Muslim government, and I was sitting in a traffic jam just outside the Pentagon. The traffic jam hadn't gone 100 yards in 20 minutes

Gary Bauer was an articulate spokesman for Christian values in six nationally televised debates during the 2000 presidential campaign.

when I got the first call about a plane crashing into the World Trade Center, which at the time people thought was an accident. Then – not that long after, which made it clear it wasn't an accident – another plane hit, and it was at that moment when I realized I was sitting at the closest point on the road that you could get to the Pentagon. I was less than 100 yards away at that particular exit and many of us in the traffic jam had our windows down. We were comparing notes – what radio stations we were listening to – when all of a sudden we heard a roar of a jet engine. I looked out of my front window and I saw movement over to the side. I turned and looked and the plane came from behind us and banked to the right and went into the Pentagon. That blast literally moved our cars, so it was a fairly dramatic moment.

I knew what had happened in New York and I had just seen what happened to the Pentagon. On the radio they were reporting there was flames and fire near the White House. There were a lot of false reports on D.C. radio stations that morning, so it was clear – in a dramatic way – that this was the most significant day that I had ever experienced.

WS: That Sudan press conference you were on your way to was going to be a very significant moment in drawing attention to what people call a holocaust or genocide that has taken place by Muslims against Christians in Sudan. Did it ever cross your mind that the timing of the attacks could have been linked to this press conference?

GB: I didn't think about the linkage, but I did think it was ironic that we were going to Capital Hill to try to pressure the Bush administration to impose some really tough economic sanctions on Sudan. It was going to be a big press conference. Probably 50 groups involved, so it is too bad that it didn't happen, but I don't think that press conference was directly related to those events that day.

Editor's note: That press conference never took place, and it took another two years before world attention was directed again toward Sudan and the slaughter there of Christians by Muslim extremists.

WS: One of the interesting undercurrents of politics in the days following the 9/11 attacks has been talk of bipartisanship and cooperation. Yet if you drill below the surface you see that the left has pushed through some controversial bills – believing that people would be afraid to oppose them.

GB: Well, you have raised two things there. First of all, on the domestic front you are absolutely right. Many conservatives in congress have concluded that we had better stay away from the controversial issues like the sanctity of life or opposing the gay rights agenda because those are distractions right now.

Unfortunately, the Ted Kennedys of the world and the Barney Franks of the world and the Hillary Clintons of the world haven't decided to do the same and they have been pushing legislation to extend benefits to same-sex couples and a number of other things.

The elected officials who identify with our cause need to wake up to the fact that there is still a cultural war going on even though we are also involved in an international war against terrorism.

On the Colin Powell issue, almost every time in our history when we are at war, there have been splits within the governing administration. There is a split in the Bush administration, Vice President Cheney and Secretary Rumsfeld tend to be in the branch of the administration to be tough and firm and want to fight this war, and not the way we fought Vietnam, with one hand tied behind our back. Powell, unfortunately, is in reality much more of a peacenik. When I was in the Reagan administration, Colin Powell fought adamantly to get out of Ronald Reagan's famous Berlin speech the most important line, which was: "Mr. Gorbachev, tear down this wall." Powell said it would insult the Russians and

Gorbachev. After a weeklong battle, the President finally just told him it's a closed issue. Reagan said, "That is why I am giving this speech, to say that line." Colin Powell was the one that talked them into not finishing the Gulf War and taking Saddam Hussein out of power.

WS: What do you think his motivation is for that?

GB: Gosh, I find it harder to get inside someone's heart or head. He's no doubt a decent man, but I just think he is wrong on these sorts of issues. He is also now the head of the State Department, where there is great sensitivity always about the concerns of other nations are but often but not as much interest about the interest of the USA. So in some ways I think his bureaucracy is sort of his directing what he does on these issues.

WS: Today the issue is not so urgent, but a couple of years ago, when the U.S. was debating most favored nation (MFN) status for China, you were perhaps the most outspoken opponent. MFN was ultimately approved, and we haven't heard much about it recently. But I can't help but observing that during that time you were almost a lone voice.

GB: I think we do have a major problem with our China policy and once you give them most favored nation status it becomes very difficult to take it away. It is clear they are using the money from trade to build up their military, which means down the road another American president is going to find himself/herself in a difficult situation.

WS: Are you glad you ran for president?

GB: I am glad I ran. Obviously this was a life changing event. I was very comfortable at the Family Research Council. I could have put in another 10 or 15 years and have a good retirement. I risked a lot doing this. On the other hand, I was at 5 or 6 national debates. I was able to press the leading candidates on issues that really matter, including the sanctity of life. I got known by a lot of people who previously didn't know about my work and, interestingly, today when I travel I am stopped by Christians who thank me for running, and that is very heartening for me. I am stopped by people who will say, "You know what, Mr. Bauer, I am not a Christian, conservative, or a Republican, but I have to tell you, you really made me think about some issues that I had not thought about before in this presidential debate." So if we had that affect and maybe kept Bush on the right path on a couple of issues, I feel like it was worth it, even though my family went through a lot. It's a nasty business. There were a couple of mornings when I would have preferred to pull the cover over my head than get up and face the day.

WS: I think it was Adlai Stevenson who said "any man who would do the things necessary to become president is unfit to serve" or something like that. Was that your experience?

GB: Reagan is my model. I worked for him for eight years. He tried three times for the presidency. In fact, two of the times he tried he failed so badly no one remembers. But eventually he won two terms. I don't see any reason to run to try to make a difference if all you are going to do when you get the nomination is be milk toast.

WS: Does that mean you are going to run again?

GB: Oh please. I am going to stay in politics and government and we will see what happens down the road. The other day on Fox News I announced a new project called the Citizens Committee To Win The War. Remarkably, within 10 hours we got over 2,000 phone calls. That will take up a lot of my energy and time in the years ahead.

WS: One more question about the presidential race, and that relates to the way you got out of the race, by throwing your support to John McCain.

GB: I surprised people and probably disappointed people.

WS: I think you did disappoint a lot of conservative Christians and I guess my question is what was your thinking there? Do you regret that decision? Not only because of where McCain stands on the issues, but because if you had supported Bush you could be sitting on the cabinet today?

GB: First, even the competitors of the race that did come out strongly for Bush are not in his cabinet. That is an interesting observation, really, on the president. The Bush family has not tolerated competition very well over the years. I did expect to see Steve Forbes and Alan Keyes and people like Elizabeth Dole in the Bush cabinet, and none of them are because at one point they were rivals.

Secondly, I welcome the opportunity to explain why I made that endorsement of John McCain. When I dropped out of the race, it was a toss up. I don't believe either of them are as conservative as I am and I don't think any are as pro-life as I am. I met with them privately and I asked for one thing in exchange for my endorsement, and that was a private commitment that if they were elected president and there was a Supreme Court vacancy, that their judicial nominee would be committed to overturning Roe vs. Wade and ending abortion. Gov. Bush would not then make that commitment to me. Sen. McCain did and in the presence of several witnesses, including a couple of Christian members of Congress. Now, he could have been misleading me. He could have reneged on it after he won, but even though I knew I would take a lot of heat, that it was worth taking a chance, particularly since some pro- life and pro-family leaders had endorsed Bush.

Also, if McCain had become president, we would have been shut out, so I felt it was worth getting a foot in the door, particularly in view of that commitment. I have been disappointed with McCain on a number of things he has done since the election is over. I think he has made a couple mistakes on a couple of issues, but knowing what I knew then and given that I got that commitment from him, I would have done the same thing.

WS: Sean Hannity recently said that if we had nine pro-life Supreme Court justices today, it would still take ten years to overturn Roe vs. Wade. He said don't give up on Roe, but that this is a battle for the hearts of the American people. He said the reality is Americans are not pro-life to any sort of depth. Many Americans in fact support the current policies on abortion.

GB: Sean is a good guy, but that is a pretty depressing message. I disagree with him. I think the American people are certainly more pro-life than the law is. The law represents a radical view of abortion on demand during all nine months of the pregnancy. You can't find more than 10 to 15 percent of the American public who thinks that ought to be law of the land. I think hearts and minds have moved a great deal. I also disagree with him about Roe vs. Wade. Two good Supreme Court appointees by Bush and this could happen in the next two years.

WS: But then you have to wait for the right case and then it has to work its way through. I think that was more his point – that it can take a while.

GB: You know, there are always these cases bubbling up and if you got a couple good appointments it would not be hard for the court to encourage those cases to come to it.

WS: Speaking of judicial appointments, apparently Patrick Leahy and the Judiciary Committee has has blocked more of President Bush appointments in the first year of his presidency than any other Judiciary Committee in history. What does that say about the process?

GB: It says a couple of things. It says that liberal Democrats play hard ball and I don't know how long it is going to take for my party to discover that we can't play by gentlemen's rules when they are going to play by back alley rules. We confirmed Bill Clinton's judicial nominees left and right and many of them should have not been put on the court. The best thing to do at this point is for the president to publicly complain about this point consistently. Do it every week, because most Americans don't know his judicial appointments are being held up. The second thing to do on Supreme Court nominees is line them up. Find five, six, seven, eight people – all of them we're willing seat on the court, and be prepared to lose a couple of them. I think if you nominate a solid conservative, pro-life jurist and the senate votes him down and you send up another and the senate votes him down and then a third – at some point the senate will blink before the president has to blink. If they are voting people down on the basis of ideology I think the public will react to that. There will be a backlash a lot faster than there would be a backlash against the president as long as he is sending up qualified people that don't have any ethical tax problems or so forth in their background.

WS: Obviously we have this war we are in right now, but what is next for the culture war? What should Christians be most concerned about of the issues that are coming over the horizon.

GB: Certainly restoring protection to unborn children has got to be a major focus. Another issue is resisting the demands of the gay rights movement. You know there is a horrendous effort under to redefine marriage so that men can marry men and women can marry women. It is just incredible to me that we are having a debate about this. I don't think the American people would ever vote for it. But judges can force it on us. We have to do everything we can to resist this.

A Platform For The Family

Ken Connor

*W*hat would cause a successful trial lawyer – with a solid chance to become the attorney general of Florida – to give it all up to lead a non-profit organization? Well, it helps that the non-profit is the Family Research Council, one of the most influential pro-family organizations in the nation. Ken Connor served the FRC for three years before returning to private law practice and book-writing. His first book, "Sinful Silence: When Christians Neglect Their Civil Duty," was published in 2004. He now takes on cases, especially those involving abortion and other life issues, that have a chance of shaping public policy.

Warren Smith: When you took over leadership of the FRC, it was to take the place of Gary Bauer, who left to run for president. How do you feel about stepping into that role at this point?

Ken Connor: Well, for a fellow who is small in physical stature, Gary left big shoes to fill. He's a brilliant advocate and insightful politician and I thought he did an extraordinary job in leading the Family Research Council. I was convinced to leave my own job and to pursue this role out of a great conviction that the platform for influencing public thought and ideas and issues was extraordinary and couldn't be duplicated in many political offices. So as a person who is passionate about cultural change, I was looking for a way to spend the rest of my of my work life, and after considering running for political office, I felt like the platform at FRC actually offered greater potential for changing the culture.

WS: You ran for governor in Florida, and you were seriously thinking of running for attorney general in Florida, and a lot of people thought you could have won that race. In many states the attorney general's job is a stepping stone to the governor's chair. But you really think being president of the FRC gives you a better chance to impact the culture?

KC: I really do. Otherwise I would not have taken it. The position of president at FRC offers a very broad platform to talk to policy makers, opinion leaders, media, and ordinary people. The range of issues is really extraordinary.

WS: I did want to talk more about those issues, but before we move on, let's talk a bit about the FRC. Even though Gary Bauer was a great leader for many years, during the time he ran for president the FRC, at least from a financial point of view, went into a bit of a decline. From 1998 to last year income was off a good bit. Has that affected what the organization is able to do, and what are you doing to address that?

KC: You're right about the change in income. FRC was without a public leader for two years. I think the amazing thing is that it sustained at the high level that it did, which shows first of all excellent internal leadership and a commitment to mission and a recognition on the part of its donor base that FRC was carrying out its mission. This has been a very tough year for all non-profit organizations, but at FRC we are actually ahead of last year, while some very fine organizations who are performing important work are behind their previous fiscal year. So we feel fortunate that we are ahead. We are not at the level we want to be or expect to be, but we feel like we are making progress.

WS: You said tonight, and I get a sense from watching other Christian groups, that we do a pretty good job saying what we are against, but not so good a job at articulating what we are for. What are you doing to articulate a positive vision for the FRC?

KC: That is accurate. But in fairness, in the past with the Clinton administration many conservatives had to stand up against

Ken Connor was one pro-family opposed to a Defense of Marriage Amendment (DMA) because it "doesn't go far enough." Insiders have suggested that he left the Family Research Council after only 10 months as president because of his stand on this issue, which brought him into conflict with Dr. James Dobson and other advocates of the DMA.

things they were opposed to. Now in Washington we have an administration that is sympathetic to the family. Sympathetic to the sanctity of life. And what we want to do is cast a vision for America that will lift people and point them to transcendent truth and propel them to make personal sacrifices for the greater good and so we are increasingly talking about what we are for because we are in an environment that permits us to do that, and we haven't been in that environment for some time. We want to help President Bush cast a vision for America that will inspire and motivate people to reclaim that vision of being the shining city on a hill that President Reagan talked about.

WS: A lot of conservatives are heartened that Bush, who many consider to be a pro-life conservative, is in the White House. On the other hand, it is sometimes good for organizations like FRC to have a devil – so to speak – to fight against. Now that conservatives are in the White House, is the movement going to get mushy and move to the middle to keep power, or are organizations like the FRC going to press their agenda even harder?

KC: My hope is that this is the dawn of a new era – the post Clinton era – where public policy will reflect an appreciation for the role of the family. The danger is that conservatives will presume that because we won the election that the battle is over. Nothing could be further from the truth. It's only the beginning. The danger is that we become apathetic, thinking the situation is well in hand.

The beachhead that Bush has established with his election is very much in jeopardy. The shift of power in the Senate reflects that. There are many who think the president lacks the verbal fluency to make the case. I don't think that is true. He has demonstrated through his acceptance speech at the convention, and through his state of the union of speech, that he has the capacity to cast a vision and to inspire people. He has a phenomenal speech writer. But the biggest asset he has going for him is that he is regarded by most Americans as a man of great integrity and sincerity and the public likes him. He is able to use good humor to his advantage. I think because of his winsomeness and his sincerity and genuineness he can deal with some difficult issues in a thoughtful way, a way which doesn't scare the public. No one can call Bush a radical. He isn't a flamer. He can talk about issues like abortion, and hold children in his arms, and say, "I believe that adoption is a loving alternative to abortion and I want to protect children like this and want them to feel welcomed in our society," and people will believe it.

WS: There is any old saying that in a democracy we get the leaders that we deserve, and even if Bush does his part I guess the other side to that question is what about the American people? Even if Bush holds firm, we see that an America that is wishy washy on a lot of these issues as well. An America where folks who go to evangelical churches have higher rates of divorce than those who do not. How much will we the people expect out of Bush even if he is up to that responsibility of leadership?

KC: I am an optimist when it comes to the capacity of the American people to respond to leadership. Based on Reagan's leadership and on our response in World War I and II, based on sacrifices our founding fathers were willing to make, I think that the flame can be nurtured and cultivated in the hearts of the American people. But it takes vision. On Capitol Hill today there are any number of Bible studies that have popped up since Bush became president. People have become more public regarding their faith than they were during the Clinton administration. They feel there's an environment that appreciates and fosters those kinds of behaviors.

Besides, in the final analysis, as one of our leaders said, duty is ours, consequences are God's.

WS: The FRC and your role as the leader requires that you be media savvy, as you're talking to the media frequently. And I know you know Marvin Olasky's book *Prodigal Press,* which documents the anti-Christian bias of the news media. How do you think these changes in Washington have affected the secular press?

KC: I think that conservatives and Christians have low expectations of the media, and the media doesn't disappoint them. But too often we treat members of the secular press as adversaries and wonder why we get lousy coverage. I would attribute to media a better motive than some of my colleagues. I see them as folks who operate under tremendous time pressures, who believe they have an obligation to present a balanced view, and who – if we will stop stiff arming and are willing to listen a bit – will allow us to get our point of view out. I really don't have any complaints in the way the media treated us or the FRC. There clearly exists within the mainstream media a bias. But I found in Florida that if you treat media people as people trying to do a job and you work to help them do that job, it's amazing the positive response you get, and I found that to be true in Washington, too.

WS: You articulated areas of emphasis that the FRC will address in the coming years.

KC: The sanctity of life, the protection of marriage, the protection of religious liberty, the increased role of parents in education decision making, and family tax relief – and there are subtexts under each of those headings.

WS: Why those five? Because they form an umbrella under which a lot of things can be talked about, or because they are leverage points?

KC: Well, both. We see life as the foundation to all other rights. No other rights can exist without the right to life, and so unless we protect the right to life, the right to privacy, the right to freedom of religion, and expression, of assembly – those are booted. So protecting the right to life is foundational.

Because the marriage-based family is the cornerstone of society and virtue, we believe protecting marriage, defending the family, is critical. Family tax relief is linked to the defense of marriage. As for the others, we have seen profound hostility, especially in the judiciary, to the free exercise religion in public places. We think that is wrong and we like to see an elimination of hostility by government toward the free exercise of religion.

And our educational system has been a flop. The gap between poor children and rich children, the learning gap, is growing. Our deficiencies relative to the rest of the world in math and science continue to widen. Our current system is failing our children. We think nobody has a greater stake in educational success than parents, so they ought to have a greater role.

WS: When I was in college – more than 20 years ago – I worked briefly for a Democratic senator who was opposed to the creation of the Department of Education, and today we have a Republican president who is increasing money to the Department of Education. It seems that the center has shifted on this issue.

KC: No question about that. Bush ran as the education president. He started out with a modest but laudable set of education goals. My own fear and concern is that in the interest of declaring a political victory, the president is willing to suffer a huge defeat of his original plan, and to embrace proposals that really do little more than throw more money after the same failed practices, and so I have been profoundly disappointed at his educational agenda.

WS: What do you see as the next "big thing" coming from Washington. What I mean by that is that a year ago no one was really talking about faith-based initiatives, and now all of a sudden everyone is talking about them. What is next?

KC: What is next in terms of what will have a profound impact on the country is judicial confirmations. The president has to appoint strict constructionists who will interpret the constitution, not make law from the bench. There will be a huge fight, because the liberals love to short circuit the democratic process or get a single judge or a small number of judges on a panel to affirm their political agenda. So what's next is a huge battle for the direction of the Supreme Court and indeed the whole federal judiciary. My hope and prayer is that the president is faithful to his pledge and is willing to stand in the gap and fight for what he believes. The least accountable branch of government was never intended to be the chief architect of policy, but because the congress has abdicated its own role and has refused to rein in a runway judiciary, the judiciary has because the most equal of all branches of government. That's what's next.

Editor's Note: This interview took place in August of 2001. Less than one month later, the terrorist attacks of 9/11 occurred. Temporarily, at least, the atttention of the country was diverted from the pro-family issues Connor articulated in this interview and were focused on national security issues. Soon after that, Connor left the FRC and returned to private practice. Tony Perkins took over leadership of the FRC and has, if anything, elevated the profile of the organization even more.

But Connor's concerns here now seem prophetic, as fights over judicial appointees, including Supreme Court justices, have risen in prominence in the years since this interview took place.

Standing For The Five Pillars

Tom Minnery

*T*om *Minnery is Vice President of Public Policy for Focus on the Family. His staff produces "Citizen" magazine, a monthly issues magazine with a circulation of 75,000; Family News in Focus, a daily information and analysis radio program broadcast on approximately 1,600 radio outlets; "Teachers in Focus" magazine; Boundless, an online "webzine" for college students; and Citizen Issues Alert, a weekly fax on hot issues. In addition, the Public Policy Division trains people for effective grassroots involvement via state-based family policy councils, which now operate in 40 states, and through field seminars on specific issues. The staff also researches and publishes books, videos and position papers on a variety of public policy issues. Prior to coming to Focus on the Family, Minnery was senior editor at "Christianity Today" magazine and Capitol Hill correspondent and a manager in the Washington Bureau of Gannett Newspapers. He has a Bachelor of Science degree in Journalism from Ohio University and Master of Arts in Religion from Trinity Evangelical Divinity School. This conversation with Minnery about Focus on the Family's public policy priorities took place in his office in Colorado Springs.*

Warren Smith: As the head of public policy issues at Focus, how do you decide what issues you are going to make a core part of your activism?

Tom Minnery: The issues that we deal with emanate from one of our five pillars.

Editor's note: For a complete list of Focus on the Family's Five Pillars, see Appendix.

WS: It's interesting that evangelism is one of your five pillars, given that Focus is not directly involved in evangelistic ministry. Rather, Focus's involvement in evangelism is more strategic, in supporting parents who want to raise their children in the "nurture and admonition of the Lord." This kind of a strategy requires biblical worldview thinking, you might call it.

TM: The failure of the church to inculcate a Christian worldview is a big problem. Generally, Jesus has asked us to be righteous, and all that really means is what is right, and the first thing one needs to be right is that people need to be right with God. But that doesn't exhaust the issue of what needs to be made right. Being righteous means standing for truth, and Christian people ought to be able to stand for God's truth in whatever sphere it occurs.

Right now we are having great problems with lack of righteousness in entertainment, popular culture, and in the sphere of government. That is where the battle is raging. Too often people think of creation as Adam and Eve and the Garden, but a proper understanding of the Old Testament shows that creation involves everything. God has not allowed any part of creation to escape his mandate. The city of Detroit, Niagara Falls, the Rocky Mountains, are all part of God's creation, whether it's a natural creation or whether it's the creation of the community that subdues the Earth, which is to say, civilization. So Christians have a duty, a mandate, to be involved in every aspect of creation.

WS: How do we do that in an era where there are few or any honorable choices left? I was thinking about George W. Bush's decision on stem cell research in that context. The evangelical community was split significantly around that decision.

TM: It is troubling, but let's look at the larger picture. First of all, for whatever reason, God has mandated civil authority to be the authority we should respect. The first seven verses of Romans 13 simply says "respect authority" and the authority he was writing about – the Roman authority – was much more corrupt than we have seen today. Now, civil authority has the freedom to reject the gospel. And the civil authority not only governs Christians, but also governs non-Christians.

WS: I understand and respect that, but does that mean that we as Christians still can't stand for God's truth?

TM: Absolutely. It means that Christians should stand because we have been given the gift in this era of being citizens in a country that defines government as "of the people, by the people, and for the people." We have the inner gyroscopes to make the right decisions. Moral standards come from the Bible, and when you lose that, the only other way to have an ordered society is to point a gun. That is not freedom, but tyranny. So there is a strong connection between biblical truth and freedom.

You asked about stem cell research. Just look at where the debate is now. In the last administration we were debating about partial birth abortion. Now we are talking about life beginning at conception. This is the most powerful position that a politician of Bush's stature and profile has ever taken in American life regarding abortion. It isn't perfect because existing stem cell lines can be used for research, but he has advanced the pro-life argument profoundly, and that is why we salute him for it even though we are not fully satisfied.

Our problem is that as Christians we hold everything we believe absolutely. We believe in absolute truth, and occasionally we are not wise as we translate that into the political sphere, and I think we hurt ourselves in the pro-life movement because we have stood for what is pure. Every child has the right to life no matter how that child is conceived and so we want to see that become law. Well, it isn't going to become law. We need to have incremental gains to get back where we used to be. We have to be willing to settle for little gains at a time. Millions of children have died. We have to stop the

Tom Minnery's book "Why You Can't Stay Silent" and his leadership of Focus Action's "Stand for the Family" rallies were instrumental in creating record turnout among evangelicals in the 2004 election.

killing where we can, and not say "we won't save one baby until we can save them all."

WS: Focus on the Family is in the midst of a lot of transitions partly because of the economy, because giving is a little bit off in ministries. You have also implemented a transition plan for Dr. Dobson's eventual succession from the top spot. What do you think is the future of the ministry?

TM: I deal with public policy and I deal directly with it most days, and in terms of succession the board of directors has been planning for that for years now. With Dr. [James] Dobson's blessings, I think in the next little while people will hear voices of those who may or may not be considered to be the successor, depending on the audience. It would be inappropriate to give names now, but a year from now people will be hearing guests on the program. Dr. Dobson encourages that, because obviously he is not going to be around forever. None of us are.

WS: There seems to be an inter-generational shift in the evangelical movement in leadership. Do you see the evangelical movement, those of you who are involved in it, trying to shape the culture with a biblical worldview and not just being separatist or what have you. Are you hopeful about what you are seeing?

TM: I am very hopeful for the next generation. For the quality and quantity of Christian leaders that will be pouring into the movement. As we sit here in 2001 there are probably 25 people in the House of Representatives, who are younger, and who are there because they answered Dr. Dobson's call for Christians to be involved. Twenty years ago we didn't have that many people who are outspoken evangelicals and that careful seeding of the landscape with qualified people is continuing on a lot of fronts. We have a Focus on the Family Institute in which top college students – undergraduates – come here for a semester's worth intense worldview training. We have graduated hundreds of students and the Family Research Council has a fellowship program for undergraduate students. The Alliance Defense Fund [ADF] is defending religious freedom across the country, and doing so very effectively. They have started a fellowship for the brightest law students from secular law schools. None of this stuff existed 5 years ago.

WS: You are on the board of the Alliance Defense Fund which, as you said, is involved in legal matters. I interviewed Ken Connor of the Family Research Council a couple of weeks ago and I asked him what was next and he said judicial appointments, and it seems to me that what the ADF is doing in the legal arena is a "frontline" effort.

TM: If the ADF can influence law students into careers in the judicial branch that would be wonderful, and that is the purpose of that program.

WS: We had eight years of Clinton presidency, and a lot of liberal and revisionist judges were appointed in that time. What is to keep the left from simply stonewalling, from delaying the appointment of conservative judges almost indefinitely?

TM: That could happen. But we have been amazed at how much good we can do in hostile courts just by showing up and being prepared. For many years the ACLU [American Civil Liberties Union] has had the battle to itself, not because they have beat us every time, but because we have not shown up. Now a network of lawyers has been trained and money has been raised for good research and cases are being funded selectively. We have been surprised at how much ground we gained by being there.

WS: You have well over 1,000 employees here at Focus and it's obvious that great work is going on. You guys were instrumental in putting the Family Policy Councils together at the state level. You did this in part because in the 80s there was a devolution of power to the state level, and the state became the "front lines" in many cultural battles. We saw this in Vermont recently, in the same-sex "civil union" issue. Where do you really think the frontline battles are going to be in the years ahead, and how is the Christian community doing in response?

TM: I think without a question the frontline battle is going to be whether we can preserve marriage as an institution between one man and one woman. Who would have thought five years ago we would have been battling that, but we are – especially with the rising cases of same sex marriage. It's going to be a state by state battle, and if we lose that then I see no hope. However, I have great hope that we will not lose that battle. Who knew two years ago the State of California would have passed Proposition 22, which protects marriage. A more liberal state than California is Hawaii and that is why the gays took the battle over marriage to Hawaii. When the people of Hawaii finally got that question presented to them, they passed by a larger percent, so I have great hope that we will win that vote. I think the gays have made so many gains that they have come too far too fast and they are going to lose in the battle to destroy institution of marriage.

In This Life We Struggle

JOHN PAULK

No one has been more "out" about his homosexuality and his departure from the homosexual lifestyle than John Paulk. John's story is a spectacular one, and it is made even more spectacular by the fact that his wife is a former lesbian. But in 2000, while serving as a staff member of Focus on the Family and a board member of the ex-gay ministry Exodus International, Paulk was seen in a gay bar in Washington, DC. This began a time of reflection and healing for Paulk that he shared with the ex-gay movement in a moving presentation at the 2001 Exodus International conference. Just days after that presentation, this interview was conducted with Paulk at the headquarters of Focus on the Family.

Warren Smith: John, as we are sitting here in Colorado Springs at the Focus on the Family headquarters, you are just now, probably recovering from your travels to North Carolina to the Exodus conference. What do you think happened at that Exodus conference that may have been new and different for the homosexual recovery movement in this country and what do you see happening in that arena nationwide right now?

John Paulk: This was Exodus' 26th conference and I have been to maybe 13 conferences myself, so I have been around half the amount of time the movement has been around. I thought the conference was very different from the others for a few reasons. First, we are maturing as an organization and as a movement. In the past few years, largely due to the influence of public spokespeople, not only myself but others, we have been trying to convey a message to not only the Christian church but the secular society that homosexual recovery is valid and possible. However, in the midst of doing that

I think we have inadvertently distorted our message or had our message distorted.

WS: What do you mean by that?

JP: I think that when you communicate in a media sound bite, and they ask you, "Have you changed and overcome homosexuality?" it's hard to answer that with a yes or no because sexuality is not a black or white issue. It runs on a continuum. I don't care who you are, there is a continuum to sexuality, sexual struggle, sexual temptation, behavior, what have you.

I think what we have done in our movement is to respond the way the media wanted us to respond by saying, "Yes, I have changed. It's all washed up, and I am done with it, and now it's packaged and pretty. Here's my wife and two beautiful children."

I think we have realized the failure of this kind of answer. The leaders – myself included – need to say that in this life you may struggle, but God can give you victory over struggle. This is the paradox, that we can live a victorious life in the midst of struggle. And that is what I saw at the conference. I saw maturity in the answers and the responses that were given by people. I saw more of a focus on spiritual work in someone's life, not just behavioral change. The theology that was coming out was what I considered to be more correct.

WS: Speaking of theology, in the movement there has been two strains or streams. One stream in the homosexual recovery movement believes what you are saying, that sexuality is a continuum and that in this life we do struggle, but that Jesus offers victory over these struggles. In this life the process of sanctification is ongoing. And there are others – often those who come out of a Pentecostal background – who say that when you're healed, you're healed. There's been some tension in the movement regarding this issue, and those on the outside of the movement have exploited this tension, or called attention to those who at one time said, "I'm healed"

For more than a decade, **John Paulk** was perhaps the nation's most prominent "ex-gay" spokesman and activist.

and then later stumbled.

JP: I have been on the board of Exodus International for six years. My term just ended last week, so I know that the point of view of Exodus as an organization is that healing is an ongoing process, just as sanctification is. When you're born again, something happens supernaturally to take care of your eternal destiny, but sanctification and healing are processes you will go through the rest of your life.

There are individuals in this movement who may look at it somewhat like you said. The "name it and claim it" group. Exodus does not believe that is theologically sound, although we know God has the power to instantly heal somebody. He often does. But we also know that most people don't get up out of wheelchairs, although He has the power to do that. And homosexuality is different in that it is a relational problem. It's not sexual in origin.

WS: I want to explore that idea of relationships, because some folks – like LeAnn Payne – ultimately say that the root problem of homosexuality is idolatry, our relationship with God.

JP: I would agree with that and that goes along with how God explains it in Romans 1. Paul talks about exchanging the god we worship for the one true God – the creature vs. the creator. I think homosexuality has components of idolatry.

But I don't think it starts at that place, but ends up there. We know the real issues of homosexuality start way back in childhood for most people. The desires are the end results of a lot of dysfunctions – sometimes sexual violation, molestation, peer rejection, not bonding correctly with your own gender parental figure, abandonment. That is what is at its core. It begins with the individual feeling alienated, not feeling loved, and lonely. Where idolatry comes is worshiping of other people in order to get those needs met.

WS: The reason I wanted to move in that direction is that even though organizations like Exodus and Focus on the Family work in this arena, and you have done a great deal to educate the church around the issues of homosexuality, this subject is still pretty stigmatized within the evangelical church. It seems to me that sometimes it's helpful to talk about our common sinfulness, as Romans 1 does, and the idolatry that we all engage in, rather than to focus on homosexuality. Homosexuality is just one way that we display our fallen nature.

JP: That's exactly right. That is what we have been doing the last three years here at Focus on the Family, as we have developed a department here. As a church we must get over our homophobia, if you will, and look at this issue at God's point of view and I think by and large the church is waking up a little bit to this issue.

WS: John, I know that you've already answered tons of questions on this, but I have to ask you what you have learned this past year in the aftermath of the well-publicized incident in which you went into a homosexual bar in Washington, DC.

JP: First, I have to say I began a process of coming out of homosexuality more than 14 years ago, and for a variety of reasons became one of the more prominent individuals of this movement. I think that was due to fact that my wife had been a lesbian. That was somewhat of an oddity. We both had very sensational stories. So for nine years we had been married and we had been in the public forefront and we are very vocal and thrilled that God has used us to spread this message. But that has a down side, because it feeds your ego and your flesh and your pride and all the things that are broken within you. When I came to work with Focus on the Family, three years ago, it even increased the visibility even more. People wanted me to speak everywhere. I felt like a doll that someone would wind-up and say come give your testimony, come speak here, come fly here, come fly there. In the meantime I was feeling great about my ministry. Now, this story isn't unlike a lot of Christian leaders who trip and fall into problems. I started squeezing God out of my life. I started saying, "I am pretty wonderful. Everyone seems to think so." I was squeezing God out. So a year ago I wanted to escape. I wanted to escape my life. I wanted to escape everything. My reputation. I wanted off the treadmill and I thought I wanted to go back to a gay bar. Well, of course, because God loves me he is not going to let me go out on a leash too long and I was discovered in there.

I have to say this past year has been the most difficult part of my life, but also the best year of my life – and I highly recommend it. [Laughter.] I mean I highly recommend to people to allow the Lord to take you through brokenness. I would say for several years to God, "Lord, please do what it takes to bring my life in total alignment with you." Now, I would be afraid to pray that prayer, because God did and he knew exactly what I needed – a lot of humbling and re-evaluating and re-prioritizing and realizing what was important. But I think the greatest lesson He has shown me has been about mercy, compassion, and His forgiveness. Focus on the Family stood by me, and my family stood by me like glue. Dr. Dobson had us on the radio right after this. He said that too often Christians shoot their own wounded. He said, "We are standing beside you and we believe in you."

WS: I heard that broadcast, and he did say that, but he wasn't soft on you either.

JP: No. Oh, no. Dr. Dobson was not soft.

WS: He did stand by you, but, you know, he took you to the woodshed just a bit, too.

JP: You're right. He did, and I needed that. I mean that is why he is so admired. It's been very difficult, but it has been healing. I went back into counseling. I have been in counseling for the past year, and I was fearful going to Exodus because I had been so prominent and I was the Exodus chairman of the board when all of this happened and I know I had let people down. This has been devastating to me. I said to someone the other day that working through the shame of your behavior is almost worst than your behavior. The shame. The residue. The effects.

So we had a meeting at Exodus. There is a day and half before the conference starts where all the national directors gather together. It's called Directors' Day. It's where the 100 or so directors meet and they interface with the board of directors of course and no one was saying anything. I thought someone would bring it up, but since no one did, I felt I needed the opportunity to address this crowd and I stood up and I just lost it because I felt like I owed these people who had supported me, or even those who hadn't supported me. I felt that it was just a real time to tell them what God had shown me and to exhort them at the same time, that if God has something to show you, don't wait until He has to show it to you like He did to me. I was crying and honestly I wasn't seeing how people were reacting to me. People told me afterwards that it was moving for them. For me, I just felt shame lifting off me that day and throughout the week. I felt like a little child before God again. I felt honest and real and didn't have to hide anything and it was probably one of the most healing times I ever had as a Christian and I think people saw in me a vulnerability that had not been in there a long time and I seemed approachable again and it was wonderful.

WS: Ron Elmore, who runs Beyond Imagination, [an Exodus-affiliated ministry in Raleigh, N.C.] was at that presentation and said it was an anointed moment.

JP: Well, it felt like an anointed moment. Not from me, but from God.

WS: John, a few minutes ago we talked about how the church is not very comfortable with the subject of homosexuality, and even among those who are comfortable talking about the topic, there is a range of rhetorical style. Some are strident about calling it evil and have a certain militancy in their rhetoric. Others are more pastoral.

We don't hear from them as much, but that's because the volume is a bit lower. What's the right approach?

JP: God gives us different abilities and different callings in life and he puts us in different places, but I think the best public policy on homosexuality is the power of a changed life. I think we need to lead with a redemptive message of change. Focus on the Family supports that approach. But Dr. Dobson has said that homosexuality is the defining issue for the church today, and you will know a lot about a church by where they fall on the issue of homosexuality. I think we need to get past some of the rhetoric that has alienated people. We can be very strongly against an issue, but people are behind issues. Ultimately, it's about winning people, not winning an argument.

WS: What's next for you and for Focus on the Family's ministry to homosexuals. You had six years on the board at Exodus. Now you're off the board. It's been a difficult but exciting year. Where do you go from here?

JP: My wife got elected to the board of directors, so that was exciting. To see her be elected by her peers was very rewarding not only for me to her but it gave me a sense of satisfaction. I am open to whatever God has to offer. We have a good life here. Our sons are in sports – soccer and tee ball – and we have tremendous friends here. We are loved here and so I think I am going to let my wife take the center stage right now and be proud of her.

Editor's note: In May of 2003, after more than five years with Focus on the Family, and many more years wokring with men and women struggling with homosexuality, John Paulk resigned his position as manager of the ministry's Homosexuality and Gender Department. He said, "After working 16 years on this contentious issue, it's time for me to pursue other endeavors."

You Never Know What The Future Holds

Mark Sanford

Just months after being elected governor of South Carolina, his first term, Mark Sanford has already set a course that is surprising politicians on both sides of the aisle. This interview took place in Sanford's office in the South Carolina State Capitol building in 2003. It began with a discussion of race relations, and his recent apology to the state's blacks for the infamous Orangeburg massacre.

Warren Smith: You made headlines a few months ago when you made a statement apologizing for the Orangeburg Massacre. Some are already calling your apology a defining moment in South Carolina history and in race relations. What were your thoughts as you made that decision to apologize?

Mark Sanford: A difficult concept is forgiveness. And it is predicated in many cases on asking for forgiveness. It just seems to me with so many problems around the world whether it's the Middle East, with the conflict between Jewish or Palestinian people, or in Ireland between the Protestants and Catholics. In so many different places there have been wrongs on both sides. But because nobody ever lays their cards down and says we've got to move on from here, we've got to look forward, irrespective of whose fault it was, who threw the first rock. Irrespective of that, it's important that we move on.

To begin that process I ask for forgiveness. There is nothing more disarming. If that were applied to many other hot spots around the world, it would move the ball forward. But that never happens. Instead, there is a declaration of 'you did this' or 'once you give a little then I'll give a little.' But nobody ever begins with themselves, with the Biblical concept of beginning with ourselves. I think we could gain a lot from that idea when you think about race relations in South Carolina. Have there been things done wrong by both sides? Absolutely! Rather than focusing solely who had more blame, who had more fault, the bigger picture is saying, 'I'm sorry these things happened. Now where can we go from here?' That was the purpose in Orangeburg.

WS: A couple of days ago I was with Lindsay Graham and he said that you are really shaking things up, and it isn't the Democrats that are upset about it, that the Republicans are almost as upset about it as some of the Democrats are.

MS: Our Founding Fathers set up institutions that were slow moving and methodical, fairly resistant to change. They wanted to guard against revolution, and that's not a bad thing. But it makes it frustrating when you are moving in a direction you want to go and you can't get there fast enough, but that's the way the system works. If you are indeed serious about trying to change some things, and I think there are a whole host of things that need to change in South Carolina, it does make it a little bit tough. You just have to keep pushing. There is a comfort level in the status quo in every institution – the military, business, education, politics. People get used to things the way they are. It's a very human defense mechanism.

WS: Can you talk a little bit about the president's faith-based initiatives and how those might get implemented here? Many Christians have reservations about these programs.

MS: Those very reservations caused me to vote against it when I was in Congress.

WS: And yet it passed.

MS: Right, so the money is coming. I've crossed that bridge. I

Many people think **Mark Sanford**, who served in the U.S. Congress before becoming governor of South Carolina, would make a credible candidate for president.

now have a different hat that I put on. My role in this case is to avail ourselves to public money that might come our way, money that could make a difference in some very profound ways here in South Carolina. So, we are going to work vigorously to avail ourselves of the federal money and put it to good use.

WS: The money comes in block grant form, typically. Some say turning this money into a voucher program would be better. What's your view?

MS: I would love it if that could happen because it decentralizes power and gives people more choices.

WS: Speaking of decentralization and choice, when you moved to Columbia you sent your own kids to private Christian school, and I know that some people were very excited about that decision and some people criticized you for that decision. Can you say why you made that decision? Were you trying to send a message?

MS: We weren't trying to send a message one way or another. There is a hierarchy of different responsibilities, responsibilities in terms of personal faith, responsibility to my wife, the responsibility of the father, and then responsibilities to state and federal government. Superseding my role as governor is my role as a parent and my role as a father, and we determined that our kids would get a better education there. The faith component of the school was important to us, too.

WS: You are in your early 40s. You are married. You have four kids and you joined the military when America was going off to war. If you'll forgive me for asking it this way: What were you thinking?

MS (laughing): My wife asked that question, too. Seriously, though, you have to back up. I spent six years in the U.S. Congress. I was on the International Relations Committee, and we traveled a fair bit. When you travel, you will travel oftentimes with military escorts. Often I would end up on an aircraft carrier in the Persian

Gulf or with troops in Germany, and I just became profoundly impressed with the United States military as a leadership organization. And my experiences in Congress really led me to believe that we had disconnected the rights that go with being an American from responsibilities that go with being an American. If there is anything that could bring down our civilization, it is that disconnect. And on a personal level, I wanted to be able to look in the mirror and say this is part of who I am.

There was a third component that goes straight back to my role as a father. I think what you say as a father has much less consequence than what you do. I was telling my boys that they need to serve. I don't want them to necessarily make it a career, but I want them to have some time in the military, and I thought I would have a lot more credibility as a father if I said, 'Look, at my decrepit age, I did this.' I didn't want to do it when I was 20. I wish I had done it, but I didn't. However, based on the situation, I have a lot more credibility in making that argument as a father.

WS: When you got in the race for governor, you were not originally the most pro-life candidate in the race, but over time most of the pro-life community rallied around you. Can you say a few words on how that happened, why did that take place, why did that occur?

MS: Politics is a reflection of human nature. When you get to know people, they learn to trust you or not to trust you. You take someone like Charlie Condon, with great conservative credentials, or Ken Wingate, with longtime established credentials in the pro-life community. If somebody has been in the field with you and there is some random new guy from Washington that you have never seen before, naturally it would take time. Before the governor's race, I never went outside my congressional district. The pro-life community down there is a different story. They knew me and had watched my votes in Congress.

WS: How has your faith been effective since you have been elected to this office? I know you have been in Congress, you have been in public speaking for a while, but there it was little bit different when you were in an executive position than a deliberative body in terms of just responsibility and leadership sense of weight. Has it affected your personal life? Has it affected your faith?

MS: Truman or Eisenhower said, "If you want a friend in Washington, get a dog." He was saying that as president of the United States, but I never understood that comment. I had a whole host of great friends. But they were my colleagues in Congress. Other congressmen like Steve Largent and J.C. Watts who were part of an accountability group with me. But it's different being in the executive branch. [Georgia Gov.] Sonny Perdue was here on Sunday, and he used to serve in the Georgia Senate and [said] that his old colleagues would come to him and say, 'You used to be one of our buddies, and now you aren't hanging out with us anymore.' But he couldn't anymore. He is now in a different role. I find that this is a function of being the senior executive. When you are in the legislative branch, you have many peers, but in the executive branch you do not because of the nature of the role. I find that I'm spending a lot more time in conversation with my wife, with my boys, and in prayer.

WS: It doesn't take any expert to know that four of the last five presidents have been southern governors. The other one, George H.W. Bush, was a congressman, representing a southern state. You are young. You have congressional experience, the governor experience. Any thought about what might happen after being the governor of South Carolina?

MS: It is interesting, because everyone comes at you with the crazy ideas. You ought to do this, and you ought to do that. It is very important in life, in politics, not to get ahead of yourself. One of the most valuable lessons that God ever taught me was this: The only day you've got is the day you have. You don't have yesterday, and you don't have tomorrow.

For instance, if I had planned to run for governor when I was in Congress, I would not have voted some of the ways I did. I remember a whole host of votes where it was me alone or me and Ron Paul. Votes that were not in my best interest politically, but I wasn't worried about it because I thought they were the right votes.

In my junior year in high school, I was 13th in the state in cross country. My goal had been to be number one in the state by my senior year in high school. Lo and behold, my dad gets Lou Gehrig's Disease, and it turns out that you aren't even living in the same state in your senior year in high school. Leaving aside something that is as inconsequential as how you are going to deal with cross country to deal with the larger consequence that your dad is dead. That's when it hit home for me. You can make plans, but you never know what the future holds. My goal now is simply to be the best governor I can.

Jesus In His Distressing Disguise

Jim Towey

Jim Towey was appointed in 2002 to lead the White House Office of Faith-Based and Community Initiatives. He reports directly to President Bush, and advises the president on church-state and compassion issues. Before going to the White House, Towey spent ten years as a senior advisor to Republican Sen. Mark Hatfield of Oregon and Democratic Gov. Lawton Chiles of Florida. But Towey considers his most formative experiences those he had with Mother Teresa of Calcutta. Towey met Mother Teresa in 1985 and served as her legal counsel for 12 years. This interview took place at Davidson College in April of 2005.

Warren Smith: What do you think is the biggest accomplishment you've had in this job so far?

Jim Towey: The president has changed the debate about social services in America. He has challenged the existing culture. He has branded the term "faith-based" in the public square, and he has welcomed these groups back. That is no modest accomplishment when you look at decades of relentless effort to secularize social service programs. Now you see 27 governors with faith-based offices. You see over 100 mayors of the big cities with faith-based offices. So I think the president is changing the culture, changing the debate.

Secondly, because he is removing barriers so that faith-based groups can get funds, you're seeing new players get funds. Last year, $2-billion in grants went to faith-based groups. Hundreds of new organizations are getting grants for the first time.

WS: What makes faith-based programs different?

JT: Our current system often deprives [the poor] of both choice and compassion. I think it's important that we look at these issues from their perspective. In Florida, prisoners can go to a prison with a faith component and hopefully have a change of heart. Drug treatment programs now have a choice mechanism in 14 states and one tribal government, through the Access To Recovery program. We have to start asking how to better serve them, and how to encourage the healer within them. So they will want to choose life, choose health, for themselves. You can throw all the programs at the world at some people, and if that individual's heart doesn't change, it does no good. They'll stay on drugs, stay unemployed. They'll continue to ignore their children's best interests. We've got to encourage organizations that help change the heart.

WS: What's been your biggest disappointment?

JT: If we had to do it over again, early on we perhaps wouldn't have pressed for votes in Congress so quickly. But I don't have any regrets personally. Mother Teresa said that God didn't call her to be successful. He called her to be faithful. We're going to continue to press forward.

WS: Some federal programs start out with good intentions and an honorable mission but degenerate into waste, inefficiency, and even graft and corruption. What have you done to ensure that what starts well continues well after you and the president are gone?

JT: Accountability and effectiveness. Groups have to show that the money they received went to its intended public purpose. That means these agencies have to manage these grants with vigilance. And on that point, so far so good. That will never be easy, and it will require each grant to be monitored carefully.

As for effectiveness, you should never launch a program and put it on automatic pilot. If it is not effective, discontinue it. The president's budget for 2006 eliminating or decreasing the funding for some programs, and he was criticized for that. But he based those decisions on this assessment of effectiveness.

WS: Can you tell me about your own spiritual journey?

JT: I'm a Christian. The love of my life is Jesus Christ. I go to mass every morning for the strength I need to do my job as well as I can. I'm Catholic. I read Scripture daily, because I need it. The poor helped me find the Lord, back in the day. Mother Teresa often referred to the poor as "Jesus in His distressing disguise." My own journey is very much tied to the privilege I had to meet Mother Teresa in 1985, and to work for her.

WS: What took you there?

JT: I went there to meet her, but I was lost then. I saw this very focused woman, who was so compassionate. And phenomenally accessible. I thought you needed entre. I was working for a U.S. Senator, and I had a letter from him. None of that was necessary. One time, after I had been working for Mother Teresa for a while, something happened that crystallized it for me. Mikael Gorbachev was in the country meeting with President Reagan. Washington was at a high state of alert. And Mother Teresa was in town the same day. I was working on Capitol Hill at that time, and it was just an armed camp, because Gorbachev came up there to meet, and security was everywhere. And here was Mother, four miles away, and thousands of people were just mobbing her. My job was just to keep people from crushing her. She had absolutely no security. No police. Just me saying, "Give Mother some room." That was her approach to security. And that was her approach to fundraising, too, by the way. She would say, "I prefer the insecurity of Divine Providence." So she depended on God for everything. Not that people who have security details don't. But that was the contrast. She was just so approachable. She was a mother. Mothers are approachable.

WS: What do you want your legacy to be in this office?

JT: My goal is to get to heaven. Second goal is to be a good husband and father. Those two things first. Professionally, I want to be a good servant of the president. He has honored me with this job. He has been very nice to Mary and me. I have a real debt to him, and I want to do this job well.

WS: How often do you get to see the president?

JT: You know, in some ways your job is to see him as little as possible. I was just made an Assistant to the President, which is a promotion, so I report directly to him. So I see him more often. Once or twice a week. But there were times when I would see him three times a day. This week, though, he's been out of the country [at the Pope's funeral]. I was at a cabinet meeting with him on the Tuesday before he went to Rome, and he hasn't been back in Washington since. I literally try to see him as little as possible because the poor guy carries so many burdens. I'm not like Karl Rove, the chief of staff. That's the inner circle. They see him all the time. I'm not in that class.

Academics, Pastors, and Theologians

Revival And Renewal

NORMAN GEISLER

Dr. Norman Geisler is the author of more than fifty books and is one of the country's leading experts on cults. Several of his books, including "When Cultists Ask," have been best-sellers. "Legislating Morality," which he wrote with Frank Turek, won the Gold Medallion Book Award from the Evangelical Christian Publishers Association in 2002. His monumental "The Baker Encyclopedia of Christian Apologetics" has become a standard text. Currently, he is the president of Charlotte-based Southern Evangelical Seminary, which he co-founded in 1992. An annual apologetics conference hosted by Geisler and SES attracts 600 people and has grown to be the largest event of its kind. This interview took place in 2001 in Geisler's temporary office in a trailer on property owned by McKee Road Baptist Church.

Warren Smith: Why have you – and why should Christians in general – spend time learning about cults?

Norman Geisler: The number one reason is that so many people are getting trapped into them. Number two: they are dangerous. They are doctrinally dangerous, and some of them are physically dangerous. Waco. Jonestown. Some of these images are still in our minds, images of people committing suicide or going up in flames.

And in a society where cults are knocking at your door aggressively -- like Mormons or Jehovah's witnesses, for example -- literally stealing many people out of the churches -- we have to be forewarned and forearmed to handle them.

So we have a program here at the seminary, a master's degree in a cult ministries. I help people who are going to be pastors or Christian educators directors evangelistic to deal with the people trapped in the cults keep their own young people from getting into the cults and defend the orthodox Christianity against their attacks.

WS: Are you discovering in your own research or hearing from other people who are reading your works that cults are infiltrating the church?

NG: Yes, they are. For example, the Weigh-Down program, which was pretty widely reported.

WS: Are you talking about Gwen Shamblin and the Weigh-Down dieting program? She was teaching things that were contrary to the doctrine of the Trinity, I believe.

NG: Absolutely.

WS: That program is still being used in some pretty conservative and evangelical churches today, even though they know about Gwen Shamblin's statements. I guess they figure her comments don't relate directly to the course, and that as long as the course itself contains no errors, then they are at liberty to use it. How do you differentiate a cult from someone or a group that is merely in error about a single or a few doctrinal points?

NG: First of all, this was no small point. They were denying the Trinity.

As for a definition, let me say that there are social and psychological dimensions to cults. But a cult by definition denies one or more fundamental Christian doctrines, such as the divinity of Christ, the Trinity, the atonement, bodily resurrection, salvation by grace.

WS: T.D. Jakes is very popular in the evangelical world, and some people say he denies the doctrine of the Trinity.

NG: That' s correct. He does. It's an old, old heresy in the Christian church called modalism. I know T.D. Jakes is very popular, and I know people don't like his ministry being called a cult, but it is. It would have been condemned by any orthodox church down through the centuries.

WS: What does it say about the evangelical church that these

Dr. Norman Geisler is one of the world's leading apologist for the Christian faith. He is founder and president of Southern Evangelical Seminary.

heretical teachings have been allowed to creep in so readily, and even when they are identified as extra-biblical, or cultic, a lot of evangelicals just wink?

NG: It says the evangelical church in America is about 3,000 mile wide and an inch deep. Doctrinally, we are very shallow. In North Carolina we are in what is called the Bible Belt, but our problem is that we don't have enough Bible under our belts. We have enough religion to makes us susceptible, but not enough doctrine to make us discerning. You can't recognize error until you can recognize the truth. I'm told that when government experts want to train people to recognize counterfeit currency, they study genuine currency. The same is true with doctrine.

WS: The Brownsville Blessing movement, and the Toronto Blessing movement. Believers in those movements claim there were manifestations of gold dust. Even a lot of charismatics started distancing themselves from those movements when the gold dust claims started being thrown around. Yet many people are very ready to embrace that sort of thing.

NG: Because, as P.T. Byrum said, a sucker is born every minute. And in America, you can change that to a sucker is born every second. Yes, there are cultic tendencies in the evangelical churches. The "Jesus-only" movement denies Father and Son, and that is a cult by definition because it denies a major doctrine. And you have the radicals in the Word of Faith Movement who are saying that God the Father has a body. The Bible says God is spirit. That's denying a major truth about God. You even had Benny Hinn saying there are nine persons in the trinity -- three in the father, three in the son, and three in the holy spirit. He later he backed off that. He said this was a revelation from God. Well, if it was a revelation, either God was wrong or Benny Hinn was wrong. Then he said Jesus didn't atone for our sins on the cross. He had to go to hell to finish the job. Incredible things infiltrating the evangelical church, to say nothing of the real notable cults outside of us. And the reason gets back to our failure to emphasize doctrine, our failure to teach the word of God to people and to instead emphasize experience.

WS: Other than deep study on the part of pastors and other leaders, are there other possible solutions? By that I mean to ask what the role of church polity and church discipline is?

NG: Well, first it's a lack of doctrinal depth. Secondly, it's a lack of doctrinal discernment. And thirdly it's a lack of church discipline -- and in that order, because if you don't know what doctrines your church policies should enforce, what you have is really just a hymn-singing Rotary Club; it's not really a church. We need strong doctrine. We need to be very discerning about it, so that when people deviate from it the courage to discipline is there.

WS: You are president of an evangelical seminary. What have you accomplished and where do you want to go in the next year or two?

NG: Well, as a matter of a fact, what we have been discussing is at the center of our mission. This is our purpose: to preach the gospel and defend the faith. Defend the faith internally and externally and that includes from all the cults and all the forms of religion. So we have a master's degree in training people to do that very thing, to defend the faith and to discern what is a cult and what isn't and to minister to people who are trapped, and to keep others from getting trapped.

Now, in a city that has six seminaries you would think that another seminary wasn't needed, but the reason that we exist today is because -- to put it in market terms -- we have a niche in the market, and that niche is there because by conservative counts there are at least 1,000 and probably 3,000 cults. The Watchman Fellowship alone has 10,000 files on people or cults so they are proliferating and where they are proliferating. The seminaries are not dealing with them. There are very few seminaries that have master's degrees on cults. You can count them on one hand. In fact, the ones who are doing exactly what we are doing you can count on one finger.

So that's why we exist today, because we have a niche and we are training people and they are coming from all over. We have 3,000 inquiries from 49 states and 15 countries, and we have no national advertisement. It's word of mouth, or people find us on the Internet and they say, "that's exactly where I want to come."

God has given us and we have just bought about 10 acres. We have a million-dollar matching gift, and we have already raised $200,000 of that. We have over 200 students here, and an internationally known faculty that have written 150 books. They are drawing students, too. People like Ravi Zacharias and Ron Rose. And people like Josh McDowell, Hank Hanegraaff and John Ankerburg are all on our advisory board. They all recommend the seminary to people.

We have the property and we are going to continue raising the million dollars for the matching gift, and then we are going to start building. Hopefully by the end of the year we can start on the building. Our goal is to train trainers and to disciple disciplers. If you teach students, it stops there. But if you teach teachers it never stops. If you train a trainer it never stops.

Editor's Note: More than $3-million was ultimately raised and Southern Evangelical Seminary now occupies a 40,000 square foot building in south Charlotte. More than 400 students now attend the school.

WS: What do you think the state of seminary education in the country is today?

NG: In one sense it's very encouraging. When I started in the ministry 51 years ago there were only a handful of good seminaries and now there are 100 or 200 of them. So in one sense it's good. In another sense, seminaries are subject to some of the same things churches are, going experiential or going "how to" instead of "what" or "why". We are teaching them how to preach, but not what to preach. We see some seminaries with courses that might as well be in basket weaving. What we end up with churches that have programs that would succeed even if there was no God!

WS: It sounds like you are making a not so subtle indictment on some of the targeted, methodologically driven churches that we are seeing spring up in the area. Am I reading too much into that comment?

NG: Well, I am not opposed to being "seeker-sensitive," but I am opposed to being seeker-centered. It should be God centered, and Bible based.

WS: Of course, people involved in seeker-oriented ministry would never admit that they are not God centered. How can you know whether they are – or for that matter, whether you and I are -- or not?

NG: By the book of James. I don't see them taking people from a lower level of knowledge and faith to a higher level. They are not reaching a higher level. They are not teaching them to defend their faith. They say they do. They say that it's their intention. But they don't. And I have seen all the big ones.

WS: Where are your graduates going? Are they going into the pastorate? Into teaching ministries?

NG: We are conservative and we are evangelistic and we have a strong emphasis on apologetics. But we have people going to a whole range of churches from here. We have a student who is hoping to become an Episcopal priest. A Christian education director. Methodists, Baptists, Presbyterians. Some from Bible churches. Many are going into pastoral work. Many are going on to further graduate school because they want to be teachers in secular universities. We can't sit here in our evangelical bubble. We had a student accepted at Oxford. Texas A&M. St. Louis University. They're getting into good programs at the top schools. We have a student in Russia. Tony Frank is in Russia, where it's all apologetics. They don't believe in a soul, let alone God. You have to start with pre-evangelism.

WS: If what you say is true, that there are a good deal more good seminaries today than there were 50 years ago, but the culture is not a good deal more Christian, what is going wrong?

NG: That's an interesting question. We are better trained than we were 50 years ago. We have better schools and we have more schools. We have a higher level of education in the ministry and in the people in Christian work. But for a full generation or two, depending on how you measure it, we withdrew from the culture. "Fortress Fundamentalists," Carl Henry called it.

WS: What more needs to happen if Christians are to have a significant impact on the culture?

NG: We need two things. We need a revival and a reformation. One won't do it. You can't reform people who are not revived, and just reviving people is just not enough. Only then can we begin to make institutional changes.

WS: By institutional changes, do you mean within the churches, or within the government?

NG: Within the body politic and within the culture. It took a long time to get to where we are today. In 1933 the humanists signed their first manifesto. In 1934 John Dewey wrote his book about taking over the country and educational system, and in the book he said we have to make humanism the militant religion of the public schools. Between 1934 and 1961 he trained a whole generation. It took them a generation to train the leaders. But by 1961 those humanist pupils of his system had made it up to Congress and the Supreme Court. In 1961 they said humanism is officially a recognizable religion. By 1962, no more prayer in school. In 1963 no more Bible reading. 1980 no more Ten Commandment, and by 1989 you can't even teach creation.

It took 60 years. We have to do the same thing we have to get back. We have to get people's hearts, to get them to change laws and institutions, and to again penetrate the media. It will take just as long to turn it around.

WS: And you see Southern Evangelical Seminary as an instrument for that turnaround. Other than your school, do you see other hopeful indicators?

NG: I am very encouraged. Fifty years ago we didn't have organizations like the Moral Majority, or Dobson's organization. We didn't have Christian newspapers like yours. I see a lot of encouraging signs, but we have a long way to go.

WS: But it sounds like you are an optimist in this regard.

NG: I am a near view pessimist and a long range optimist. Things may get worse before they get better, but when they get better they are going to get really good. You know what a pessimist is? He is someone who feels bad when he feels good because he is afraid if he felt better he would get worse.

So I am not a pessimist.

A Bridge Between Two Worlds

HADDON ROBINSON

Haddon Robinson was named in a Baylor University survey as one of the 12 greatest preachers in the English language. A professor at Gordon-Conwell Theological Seminary in South Hamilton, MA, he has also developed a reputation for being one of the nation's leading teachers of the art of preaching. We wanted to find out what makes great preaching, what the state of preaching in the evangelical church is today, and the state of the church itself. This interview took place in 2001.

Warren Smith: What was it about the preachers on the list that made them great?

Haddon Robinson: To be honest, the people on the list are for the most part, people who have published. Therefore, when 1500 were asked to name these people, they named them. But I don't think they sat down and listened to us preach and said, "There's a great preacher." I think they read what we wrote about preaching.

But what makes a great preacher? In the Baylor survey, the first qualification is that a great preacher is someone who communicates well, is able to connect. Is audience oriented. Another thing is that great preachers have strong ideas. They are known for having something important to say, and they say it well. They have good delivery. By that, they say what they have to say in a way that draws people in. Of course, I think a really good sermon draws its great ideas from scripture.

So, great ideas communicated in a relevant fashion in a way that gets the audience to listen and apply it to their lives. That's what makes a great sermon.

WS: Given those standards, how would you characterize the state of preaching in the evangelical church today?

HR: On the whole, I would say that preaching is relatively weak. There are marvelous exceptions. But I don't think people on the whole when they go to church are forced to think outside the categories they are forced to thinking in, that they are challenged.

Of course, sometimes that is the fault of the audience. If a preacher challenges the way people think or act, sometimes the audience won't accept that. They become angry or upset. I think sometimes it comes because preachers often have to speak three times a week – Sunday morning, Sunday evening, and in the middle of the week. Nothing significant can come out of your mouth unless something significant is going on in your head. And if you have to preach not because you have something to say, but because you have to say something, then you fill the time. In that case, it is practically impossible for someone to have a thought that develops out of an understanding of scripture, and an understanding of how that biblical concept applies to people in the 21st century.

I think another reason preaching is weak is that pastors are expected to do everything. They are not only communicators, but they have to be chief executive officers of an organization. They have to be grief therapists. They're expected to be counselors. People who are hurting come to them, and they have to be able to interact appropriately. They're expected to be Christian educators, to provide an educational program that touches everyone from the womb to the tomb.

So if you look at all of this, even though the pastor may want to be a preacher, often the business of his life keeps that from happening.

WS: It sounds as though you're making a case for increased specialization of function for the pastor – which some would argue necessarily implies a certain size or scale of the church. In other words, before you can have that kind of specialization of function, you must have three or four or five people on staff who handle

Haddon Robinson: "It ends up that the pastor suffers from vocational amnesia. He doesn't know who he is. He doesn't know what he is supposed to do. And, of course, thinking is hard work. So it is easy to be tempted to do other things, rather than to study."

these various functions. Besides, is it such a bad thing that a pastor is a grief counselor, or an educator, as well as a preacher. It seems to me that this kind of integration of skills and diversity of life experience in one person is not a bad thing.

HR: You're right. It's not a bad thing. It ends up, though, that the pastor suffers from vocational amnesia. He doesn't know who he is. He doesn't know what he is supposed to do. And, of course, thinking is hard work. So it is easy to be tempted to do other things, rather than to study.

WS: What do you think about the pressure on preachers to be entertainers? That tends to discourage lay leadership in the church from rising to the occasion of being Christian educators or performing some of these other functions you have described.

HR: One solution is for lay people to do many of the very things that the pastor is now called upon to do. This requires a leader who is able to delegate, and people who are willing to be delegated to! That is why smaller churches do important work, and are often outstanding at developing disciples and leaders – because lay leaders step in and do important, even vital, work of the church. Sometimes the pastor's role is to help lay people get into the role, provide initial support, and then withdraw.

WS: There seems to be, in the evangelical world, a sense that success is equated with size. The preacher as entertainer and the worship service as entertainment seem to have taken precedence over expository preaching.

HR: I believe that any preacher that is not firmly based in the scripture is a waste of time and is in fact counter-productive because he will lead people away from God. I think the great problem that expository preaching has had in the past is that it has often not been shown to be relevant to people.

On the other hand, the topical preacher often starts with a topic that has pizzazz, goes to the biblical text merely for something to say that sounds biblical, but that's not what directs the sermon.

Strong preaching comes when flint strikes steel. When the flint of a person's question or problem strikes the steel of the Word of God. That's when you get a spark. That spark can change life.

As for the idea of entertainment, that depends on what you mean by entertainment. Just as I can read a book and be gripped by it, I can hear a sermon based on scripture, done well, and it seems to me that draws people in. The word entertainment has a negative side, but an entertainment is also something that I want to hear. When that goes on, you've got great preaching.

WS: If, as you said, the general level of preaching in the evangelical church is fairly low, don't you also have to look to the seminaries? These preachers do not spring *ex nihilo* into the pulpit. They come from the seminaries, at least most of them do.

HR: I think you'd have to say that the teaching of preaching in the theological seminaries has not been in high regard. Most schools will have two courses in preaching. Part of the other difficulty is that many people in seminary today have come to Christ in college. Many of them have not grown up in the church. As a result, when you are teaching them to preach, it's like teaching them to swim when they've never been near water. You spend a lot of time saying "That's water." And they diligently write that down.

Everyone in the group I'm teaching now here in Charlotte has been out in ministry for at least five years. They've got water up their nose. They know what the questions are. This is the most meaningful educational experience I have had in my 40 years of teaching.

It is tough to teach preaching to those who have never had to do it. The most you can do is to help them put a sermon together that is clear. But again and again, I will have students tell me that they read my book [on preaching] after they got out of seminary and had been in ministry a while, and they suddenly realized, "Aha, so that is what he meant."

So seminaries do share a bit of the blame, but there is a difficulty at teaching good preaching at the seminary level. Good preachers become good preachers outside of the seminary.

That is what is unique about this program. This is a two-week program, but there is a lot of reading they do prior to the course, and when they leave there are projects they have to do in their church. To get lay people involved in evaluating their sermons, and involved in the preparation of their sermons. To raise the questions that a layperson feels needs to be answered.

WS: So, implicit in what you are saying is that there is something fundamentally flawed about the way we've prepared people for ministry.

HR: Well, in days gone by, people would come up – be raised – in the church. So they had some awareness of what the church was, and some awareness of vital preaching. And another thing that would happen is that in years past you would graduate and go off to the First Episcobapterian Church and the people in the church knew how to do church so they would whip you into shape. They would teach you how to be a pastor by showing up, and requiring certain things of you. The elders and deacons would require certain things of you, and they were by and large the right things.

Today, because of the whole changing scene, people don't know how to do church. They don't know what a church should be about to touch people in the 21st century. Even though they may say that preaching doesn't touch my life, they don't have a ghost of an idea about what might be done differently. So you don't get the post-graduate education in churches that you may have 40 years ago.

WS: Yet I heard as recently as yesterday that the majority of people who come to Christ come to Christ before the age of 12. And yet you are saying that many of your students in seminary are people who came to Christ in college. Help me reconcile these two data points.

HR: The mass of people who are Christians were brought up in a Christian home, and do have a childhood experience of faith, but if you ask even those children, you will discover that they had to go through an experience in which that faith had to be confirmed. Whether you are a Baptist, or a Presbyterian, or a Lutheran, or whatever. The faith of a five-year-old will not sustain that child as he approaches adulthood. The testimony is usually something like this: "I trusted Christ when I was six, but I drifted away, and when I got into my teens I went to youth camp and re-dedicated my life to Christ."

Well, it is in that area of re-dedication that I think sometimes they actually became a Christian. They were nurtured as a young child, but the meaningful decision to follow Christ came when they realized what this was all about. That is why I say that it is often in late high school or college where most people who are Christians as adults say that Christ got a hold on them.

WS: If what you say is true, and if it is also true that most people don't know how to do church, and the environment in which they do start wrestling seriously with Christ is more likely to be youth camp than church, how do they learn the liturgy, the catechism – those things that some disparagingly call form and ritual, but in its way is didactic and does teach important doctrines of the faith. Or are these forms merely relics of the past?

HR: If a church does traditional things, they had better do them well. You can do contemporary worship much less well. Why? Because contemporary forms are already a part of what people are. But traditional forms are not, and the risk is seeming irrelevant. If you sing 300-year-old hymns, with words that are very different from the words you hear every day, there had better be excellence and beauty in those words. Contemporary forms do not carry that burden.

What those of us who are in leadership have to face is the fact that people coming to church today do not have even the most basic understanding of the facts of the Christian faith. I was flying on an airplane some time ago, and the fellow sitting next to me found out I taught at a seminary. That's usually the kiss of death to a conversation, but this fellow wanted to know more. He asked me: "What's Christmas?" I said, "It's when we celebrate the birth of Jesus." He said: "What's Easter?" I said, "That's when we celebrate the resurrection of Jesus." He said, "What do you mean by resurrection?" I said, "We believe that Jesus was murdered and put in the grave and three days later he came back from the dead."

He said, "Do Christians believe that?" I said, "All Christians should believe that." He said, "That's interesting. I think I knew about Christmas, but I didn't know about Easter."

Think about that. In our culture, you can learn the basics of Christmas. But where would you learn the basics of Easter from pop culture? There's no Easter music on the radio. This fellow grew up in the United States. And we have more and more people like that with each passing year. If we expect them to learn liturgy before they can worship with us, they're not going to make it. We're not in a post-Christian world. We're really in a pre-Christian world.

Think about that. When the apostles went out, they went into the synagogues. And in the synagogues, they could preach the Old Testament to people who believed the Old Testament, and out of that there would be those who would be converted. Then they hit the marketplace. Today, in many areas of the country, we don't have those people who might be called synagogue people. We are going to a mission field, and if we don't have a mission field mentality, we're not going to reach them.

WS: I'm aware of Lesslie Newbiggin's essay, "Foolishness to the

Greeks," in which he described the remnants of western culture as the new mission field. But I also read that 40 percent of people say they did attend some worship service in the past week. Of course, there is also other data that says when you ask people this question, at least half of them will lie!

HR: Yes!

WS: And there is a Barna survey that says people who identify themselves as born-again don't believe in the resurrection, or the virgin birth, or other key doctrines.

HR: Well, part of the issue is that when you and I use that term, "born again," we fill it with meaning. But lots of people use that word in ways that you and I don't. It describes spiritism, or some experience that is semi-religious, perhaps, but has nothing to do with trusting Jesus Christ. Has nothing to do with John 3.

WS: I guess that's my point. It seems that disciple making has to be more than self-referencing. It has to be based on sound teaching. Jesus said, "Go and make disciples." He said that to his disciples. What does that look like today?

HR: The Great Commission's major verb is "go and make disciples." You do that by reaching them, baptizing them, and teaching them. I think our task is to take men and women who are not Christians and bring them into a relationship with Jesus Christ, and have them grow in that relationship until they develop maturity in their relationship with the Lord Jesus.

WS: It seems that people are being reached, but they're not being taught.

HR: That's the great danger. Many contemporary churches are doing a great job or reaching people, but they face frustration when it comes to making them fully committed followers of Jesus Christ. I admire these churches because they have been effective at reaching people who do not ordinarily come to church. We can learn a lot from them. But many of them are evaluating what they are doing, because they are realizing that what they have been doing is not enough. We have seen this evolution in the church -- from traditional to evangelistic to disciple-making – all of this has taken place in the past 30 years.

WS: Well, then let's go back 30 or 50 years. Billy Graham was coming along with Youth for Christ. Campus Crusade just celebrated its 50th anniversary. The Navigators, InterVarsity. Right after World War II there was an explosion of these types of para-church organizations. The ground was fertile for these organizations. Perceptive people say they sprang up because of a failure of the church. My question is: shouldn't there be some sense of urgency about recovering what was lost in the church, rather than turning the church into a para-church group.

HR: I think what happened 50 years ago was the great liberal-fundamentalist controversy. Liberals won. They won the denominations. What you had 50 years ago was a transformation of fundamentalism to evangelicalism, in the sense that they said, "We don't have to retreat and nurse our wounds. We can move out." Many churches that have sprung up in the past 50 years are a reflection of these para-church ministries. They were effective in some ways, so the churches imitated them.

I believe that today, if you look at the churches that are growing, they're evangelical. That's true in Methodism, in Presbyterianism, among Baptists, even in the Episcopal church. However, there are people for whom liturgy, in the best sense, has a strong appeal. We have a culture that is much more visual. The liturgy is visual. We have a culture that needs to hear things again and again and again. Liturgy does that. The reciting of the Apostle's Creed, and the rest.

WS: So what you are saying is that the rise of the video culture is also potentially providing fertile ground for a resurgence of liturgy.

HR: Sure. Banners in the church. Vestments. Colors to represent different seasons of the church calendar. A visual culture will respond to these things, if they are done well, and if scripture is behind them. Evangelical Anglican churches around the world are drawing huge numbers of people.

WS: If you could say one thing to a pastor about his leadership or his preaching, what would that be? What is the central message of Haddon Robinson's life and ministry to the church?

HR: I believe that the most important single thing we can do is to take the scriptures, be faithful to what they are saying, and relate them to the complex problems of people in the 21st century. You cannot just focus on problems and needs of people without an honest exposition of scripture. On the other hand, you can't stay in the 21st century BC. You've got to bring that truth to this culture.

The preacher stands as a bridge between two worlds. That takes thought and commitment. So preach the Word of God. That must be the first and deepest commitment of a preacher. There is great power in the Word of God to change lives.

Resident Aliens

STANLEY HAUERWAS

tanley Hauerwas, a professor of theological ethics at Duke University's Divinity School in Durham, N.C., has been both a comfort and a trial to theologians and Christian thinkers on both the left and the right. He is a staunch opponent of abortion and homosexuality. Yet he describes himself as a pacifist, and has been steadfastly opposed to the war in Iraq and most other military involvements of the U.S. He has also been outspoken and convincing in his criticism of the American evangelical church and its penchant for commercialism, modernism, and nationalistic tendencies. He is the author or co-author of more than a dozen books, including "Resident Aliens," which some have described as something of a "lover's quarrel" with the American church. This conversation took place in 2003 and began just moments after the great carillon at Duke University tolled 5 p.m.

Warren Smith: The subtitle of "Resident Aliens" was "For people who know that something is wrong." Say a few words about what's wrong with the church, both the liberal and the conservative evangelical church.

Stanley Hauerwas: The main problem with the American church is that it is American. I often put it this way: America was the first experiment in Protestant Constantinianism.

WS: When you say Constantinianism, what do you mean by that? Are you referring to the idea of Christian Empire?

SH: Well, it is something of a crude descriptor. But it refers to Constantine, the emperor of the 4th century, allegedly becoming a Christian. Therefore, the empire became Christian.

Everywhere Protestantism occurred in Europe it was always occurring in the context of Catholic habits, and of course they were Catholic Constantinian habits. When Protestants came to America, it seemed like a virgin country. As a result, even though the founders of the country appeared to be Christian, Americans got the idea that America was the church. Therefore, it became impossible to distinguish between being American and being Christian.

WS: So the idea is that up until then, Christians were pilgrims and aliens in the land, but they then became institutionalized in the land.

SH: John Howard Yoder, who taught me so much about this, makes the observation that prior to Constantine, Christians knew that God was active in the church, they wondered about what God was doing in the world. After Constantine, you had to accept that what ever was happening in the world was from God. Put another way, before Constantine, it took courage to be a Christian; after Constantine, it took courage to be a pagan. You can see how that changes habits.

What American Christians get confused about is the nature of the similarities. Constantine legally established the church. In America, the church is not and cannot be legally established, but it has been socially established. It is become socially disestablished now, and Christians have a lot of trouble knowing what to do with that.

WS: Given that, and if I have read rightly what you've written, the role of the church is not to impact the culture, but rather the role of the church is to be the church.

SH: Right. But, I don't want to make that either/or. The church most determinatively impacts the culture when we truthfully preach the gospel. Truthfully preaching the gospel means that Christians are people who want to know the truth about ourselves. If that were actually the case, that tendency would make wonderful contributions to the wider society. We can't expect that the wider society, who doesn't worship the God that we worship, will always be ready to do what we think we must do, but you never give up

Stanley Hauerwas: The problem with the American church is that it is more "American" than it is "church."

hope. One of the problems in America is that Christians think they need everyone to do what we believe they should do in order for us to be who we are. But our path is to be who God has called us to be, whether anyone else is that way or not.

For example, I am a person who feels very strongly about abortion. I just don't think Christians can abort children. I think the abortion policies of this country are awful. I would very much want to find ways to serve my neighbor in a manner that would make abortion less likely. But in the meantime, we Christians have to get our house in order. Currently, as you well know, many Christian churches do not have a problem with abortion. How that argument occurs among ourselves is important.

WS: How should that argument occur?

SH: Well, those churches who are OK with abortion have become more democrat than Christian. For example, take the language, "I have a right to my body." Where did that language come from? It came from democratic liberalism. That's not Christian language. Where did Christians ever get the idea that they have a right to their bodies? Our bodies are gifts from God. We don't have a right to them. Christian discourse has become so invaded by democratic speech, often a very debased democratic speech, that Christians have a lot of trouble even understanding why we're different.

WS: But the religious right doesn't get it right, in your view, either.

SH: The problem with the religious right is, again, that they identify Christianity with America. Think, for example, about the use of the American flag in the church. The American flag shouldn't be in the church. That's idolatry. The American flag represents the significant sacrifice that people made have made for this country. I respect that sacrifice, but that's precisely the problem. It's such a heavy moral symbol. It makes those sacrifices as important as the sacrifice of Jesus Himself. So it is harder for the world to know there is an alternative to violence.

It's very interesting that the religious right doesn't like consequentialist, utilitarian reasoning about abortion. But you hear those on the religious right justify American foreign policy with the same consequentialist, utilitarian reasoning. They say, "Of course, war is not a good thing, but sometimes you have to do it. Lesser evil, and all that." Same logic that people use to justify abortion.

WS: Therefore, you are a pacifist.

SH: I am a pacifist.

WS: Define what that really means.

SH: Well, I don't like to say I'm a pacifist, because pacifism sounds like a position that you assume separate from Christology. For me, the first thing I need to say is that I am a disciple of Jesus Christ. I think Christians would find it very difficult to justify saying that they would kill as a result of their commitment to Christ. Then, we say, well, don't kill as a result of your commitment to Christ, but out a sense of loyalty to your country. Then I say, what does that have to do with discipleship to Christ? Is loyalty to country a condition of discipleship to Christ? Then people call out Romans 13, but they do so as if it doesn't follow Romans 12. Aren't we supposed to be obedient to government? That's exactly what Catholics and Lutherans thought under Hitler. My question is this: Exactly when are Christians going to learn to say no?

So, yes, pacifism is disavowing violence as a way to achieve faithfulness to Christ.

WS: But how, then, are we to be obedient to civil authority that from time to time requires its citizens to kill? Would you say that any form of nationalism is evil? Or, perhaps more subtly, would you reject the notion that some forms of nationalism might serve the good?

SH: Nationalism is a modern phenomenon. It really doesn't develop until the 14th century. The development of the nation-state emerged as a sort of alternative to the church. And I would say that modern nationalism is quite antithetical to what it means to be a Christian.

WS: Again, though, that brings us back to the question: How should be then live in this culture?

SH: Well, we live the way porcupines make love: very carefully. Because you have to be constantly on guard to make sure that your loyalties to Christ won't be compromised by your fellow feelings. Idolatry is an ever-present danger.

WS: But there were models. The Catholic and Lutheran churches in Germany were largely co-opted by Nazi ideology, but there was also Karl Barth writing the Barman Declaration. Deitrich Bonhoeffer. Barth argued from Christology. Bonhoeffer was an activist. Not a pacifist.

SH: That's very debatable. I know a lot about that, and Bonhoeffer's resistance to the Nazis was as Christologically determined as was Barth's. Indeed, Barth was a major influence on Bonhoeffer. When the SS finally stopped the seminary at Finkenwalde, Bonhoeffer had to be protected to keep from being drafted into the army. He became, essentially, a double agent. This was when he was active in the plot against Hitler, which you were referring to. When they started to plot against Hitler, they did not want to kill him. They were desperately afraid that if they killed him, they would turn him into a martyr. So Bonhoeffer was ready to use violence against Hitler only very late, and in a very chastened mode. By that, I mean, who knows what any of us would do in such circumstances. I tell people I'm a pacifist because I'm obviously so violent. I have no faith in myself being able to live non-violently. But by creating expectations in others, I hope they will help me to live truthful to how I think I should live.

WS: So, as a consequence of all this, the church should be what? You've used the words "community" or "colony." I assume the latter is to differentiate this idea from modern notions of communitarianism.

SH: I would say a countercultural community. And I'm often accused of being communitarian. I don't like that language very much. I say I'm not a communitarian; I'm a Christian. Christian community is not just people being together to be together. They are people who are together to worship God. That means they are capable of having a lot of conflict. If you think truth matters, and I certainly do think truth matters, then you come to truth by testing out your judgments with one another, which will oftimes be conflictual. I don't know if you noticed the poster on the door of my office. It says, "A modest proposal for peace: That the Christians of the world resolve not to kill one another." Unfortunately, that's too often the case. We've got to seek the truth in order to find the truth, not just to win. This kind of Christian community is what we need in the kind of world we live in.

WS: It seems that there is another reason the world doesn't take the church seriously. It seems that this search for truth sometimes seems to be trivialized, and the church doesn't know how to respond. For example, you're a Methodist, is that right?

SH: I am, but I go to an Episcopal church right now.

WS: Well, that makes my point even more. Because if the Methodists have a few problems, the Episcopalians have a few more. Bishop John Spong, for example. Bishop William Swing....

SH: They should have been tried for heresy and kicked out. Absolutely. No question.

WS: But they weren't. And what does that do to the credibility of the witness of that church?

SH: It shows that we're not capable of disciplining our own internal life. And that's a deep judgment against us. What that has to do with is how the language of tolerance has taken over

Christian communities. Christians are afraid of appearing intolerant. Methodism says it wants to be inclusive, but that's just a lie. What it means is that they will accept those who want to be inclusive only in the particular ways that they want to be inclusive. Inclusivity is a way of denying their own faith.

And that goes back to what we were discussing earlier about American Protestantism. American Protestants do not know how to give an account to authority. They think that the authority is the Bible, but the more they name the Bible as authority, the more they divide over the interpretation of the Bible. That has everything to do with the Reformation.

WS: So the Bible as authority is a form of idolatry?

SH: God should be the authority. But at some point you have to grapple with the question "which God?" American Protestants are fond of asking that question of others, while not answering it for themselves. American Protestants are all about saying "what part of all that stuff do I not have to believe?" Catholics, on the other hand, are very different. They say, "Look at all that stuff I get to believe." They have a deeper sense that the unity of the church is anchored in an ongoing tradition through which the bishops have the obligation to keep the tradition alive. That's why Catholics are not so afraid of difference. That's why I often say, "If you think an argument between an Episcopalian and a Southern Baptist is something, you should hear a Dominican arguing with a Jesuit."

WS: Yet you're not Roman. So what is the authority for you? Low Protestants argue for the Bible as authority. Catholics argue for the Magisterium. Anglicans argue for the so-called "Three Legged Stool" of scripture, tradition, and reason. Where are you on this?

SH: Yes, and the Methodists add "experience" to that. All of which just confuses things.

WS: So what's the right answer?

SH: Well, what we have to do is to recognize that we are in deep trouble as a divided church. We should be praying earnestly for unity. We've got to do that from the ground up. Most evangelicals don't have a clue as to why they're not Catholic. They may think they do, but in reality they know nothing about Catholicism. I pray for Catholics and Protestants to discover how much they need one another.

WS: So you would agree with those who say that the tragedy of abortion is a judgment against the church. It is the result of our inaction in the culture, and it is – among other things -- forcing Protestants and Catholics to work together in one of the few areas in which there's agreement so that we might learn of other areas of agreement?

SH: Absolutely. Operation Rescue, for example, is made up of evangelicals who always hated Catholics, and Roman Catholics. It's a remarkable development.

WS: On another topic that divides the church and hurts our witness: homosexuality. Can you say a few words about that?

SH: No. It's far too complex for a few words. My general view is that the church has not been effective in dealing with this because of the church's difficulty with marriage. The problems began when the church started re-marrying divorced people. That's when we got in trouble. Because we then associated marriage primarily with romantic conceptions of love and when you associate marriage with romantic conceptions of love, then – as a matter of fact – homosexual people can just as easily embody that as anyone else. The church must re-think marriage. You must remember that the first way of living among Christians is singleness. Marriage is a calling. Jesus was single. So much of contemporary Protestant evangelicalism assumes that if you don't marry, there must be something wrong with you. So we must recover a strong sense of single celibacy as part of the Christian life. People who get married bear the burden of proof in the church.

WS: You've written a bit about vocation and calling and its role as an antidote to the materialism we see in modern life.

SH: I think people are dying to have good work to do. By that I mean they are dying to make a contribution to other people's lives. When you work only to make money, it kills you. So I think that the church needs to recover a freedom for people not to succeed in conventional ways. Modern evangelical churches target the successful. But we forget that the Bible says plainly that if you have a lot of money, you've got a problem. Protestantism has rationalized that by saying, "Oh, no, it's what you do with the money." The New Testament doesn't say that. It says that if you have a lot of money, you've got a problem.

WS: As you get older, and you're 63 now, and as God strips away the dross from the gold in your thinking, what's left? By that, I mean what do you consider to be an important part of the Gospel message that you didn't really appreciate when you were younger?

SH: What's been constant with me is the importance of friendship. I think that's why God gave us Christ, to make us friends with God, and friends with each other, so that our relationships are nourishing and we are not so alone in this world. Loneliness is the besetting pathology for Americans. It's a part of the human condition, but Americans are worse because we don't want to have to depend upon anyone. Learning to be vulnerable again is crucial.

So I continue to praise God for the people who claim me as a friend. That's what the church makes possible. In the Gospel of John, at the end of Jesus' ministry, he said that before I called you disciple, but now I call you friend.

An Inch Wide And A Mile Deep

JIM WHITE

Over the past decade, Jim White has not only built Mecklenburg Community Church (MCC) into one of the largest churches in Charlotte, but he has also become a national figure in the evangelical world by writing a half-dozen books on theological and cultural issues. In the early 90s, when the church was getting national attention for its growth, I sat down with White to talk about the church growth movement and to get White's "take" on what was happening in the world and in the church. (That interview is posted on www.thecharlotteworld.com.) I visited with White again in 2003, in part motivated by the publication of White's book, "Embracing the Mysterious God," to find out what has changed – in America, in White's ministry and thinking, and in the evangelical church – since that conversation.

Warren Smith: Your latest book, "Embracing The Mysterious God," is not like many Christian books. It doesn't have "Ten Steps to This" or "Twenty Steps to That" or "Push This Button Here And You'll Get The Answer." It's not a "how to" book, which seems to dominate the Christian book list. You seem to confront both the God you can know and the God you can't know except by His grace. What motivated you to write a book about the mystery of God, which is not going to be easy for a lot of Christians?

Jim White: A lot of it has to do with my own questions and my own journey, as well as what I was perceiving to be the questions of the people I was encountering as a pastor and as a professor. When it comes to questions about Christianity and questions about God, I found that there were two basic camps, or two basic kinds of books out there. You have apologetics. Classic apologetics, which answers Enlightenment questions. Does God exist? Is the Bible true? Did the resurrection take place? We often put all of our intellectual energy into Enlightenment categories and we write books like that.

On the other hand, you have all the spiritual formation stuff. How can I get more insight into the Bible? Beth Moore. Max Lucado. How can I have a better marriage? How can I have an effective quiet time? How do I pray?

These categories are a bit simplistic, but I've found that these are the two basic camps when it comes to Christian non-fiction.

I was sensing a third group of questions that didn't fit into either of these two camps. It's a little hard to frame, but these were questions from people who were saying, "OK, I buy it. I'm in it. I'm a Christian. But, doggone it, I'm having a hard time with this aspect." It's almost as if they were saying, 'I'm married. I'm not going anywhere. But I could use some counseling, because I'm struggling with my relationship with God.'

It wasn't skepticism. And it wasn't, "How can I just pray more." It was, "OK, when I'm praying, God seems silent. What's that about? Help me process that. I'm having a quiet time, but God seems a thousand miles away. Help me with that. I'm called into Christian community, and I hate who I'm sitting next to. Everything I think I'm supposed to be doing, I'm having some tension about doing. I'm struggling with that. Can we just talk about that?"

Interestingly, I'm finding that these questions are coming from Christians and non-Christians alike. Increasingly, the questions that Christians and non-Christians have about Christianity are the same questions. Many of them came back to not "God, are you there?" But, rather, "What kind of God are you? How do I relate to you?"

As I began to answer these questions in my own life and to help others answer these questions for themselves, I kept coming back to the character of God. People are struggling with the character of God. Is this a good God or not? Am I going to trust God even if I don't understand God?

Also, I would say that I was struggling with the earthiness of the biblical materials. I went back and rediscovered their earthiness. Jeremiah saying, "You deceived me." He actually said that to God. Job. David. Abraham. Moses. They were all so direct with God. They go to God with the fullness of their lives, and they talk directly to God. They say things like, "God, I don't understand what you're doing. God, I feel betrayed right now. God, I feel like you've called me to do this, but now look at it. It's all one great big screwed-up mess."

And God didn't smite them! Sometimes He rebuked them, when they needed it. Job got a couple of swift replies. But most of the time, God said, "OK, let's talk about it." God was big enough to go there.

That's what the book is about.

WS: As a pastor, what motivated you to want to write this book now? Are you seeing the people to whom you minister in these situations?

JW: I'm seeing spiritual interest coupled with enormous spiritual confusion. Increasingly, people are open to spiritual things. They're increasingly seeing that their greatest needs are spiritual in nature. They're seeing the emptiness of materialism. So they turn themselves to spiritual things. Unfortunately, they're indiscriminate. It doesn't matter whether it's Christianity, scientology, wicca. They're spiritually illiterate. So they come with all of these feelings and this smorgasbord mentality. The result is that they come to God really messy.

We have people who come to us and say, "OK, here I am. I went

Jim White: "It's interesting that in some of the earlier books I didn't even get to choose the title. I was some two-bit, no-name kid who was supposed to be glad that they were even publishing me. And I was."

through a divorce and my life is a mess. I got invited to come to this church. Now, tell me what this Christian stuff is about." I don't think we as a culture dealt with that stuff 20 years ago. People today are coming with zero background. They don't even have a memory of the Gospel.

Earlier, I mentioned the Enlightenment. Let me come back to that. I think that in an earlier time, most people who were outside the Christian faith were outside the faith on Enlightenment grounds. They ran the Christian faith through an empirical set of truth claims and found it wanting, and rejected it on those grounds. Well, post-modern culture began to raise its head and realized that the Enlightenment was found wanting. Christians could applaud that. You're right. Science isn't God, and the supernatural realm is alive and well. What we weren't prepared for is that post-moderns didn't embrace Christianity. They went from the Enlightenment to something that motivated questions we've never dealt with before. Now, it wasn't "Is the Bible true?" It's now, "What is truth?" It wasn't "Did Jesus rise from the dead?" It's, "So what if He did?" We never had to answer those questions before. And we started giving them Enlightenment answers again, and they're saying, "Oh, please. I'm going to go watch 'The Matrix' again."

WS: And they say that because "The Matrix" touches the mysterious in some way that we are not. Are you saying that even though Christianity has the source of ultimate mystery, we're denying that?

JW: Exactly. We don't know how to convey that. We don't know how to help them approach that mystery. We don't know how to scratch them where they're itching. There's a disconnect between the truth that we have and the questions that they're asking. That is always an ongoing challenge. How do you bring the truth of Christianity to bear to the culture of that day.

By the way, I think that's why people were so disappointed with the second and third "Matrix." The first one raised hope and interesting questions. But when people got the answers, they said, "Well, that stinks. That doesn't satisfy."

But going back to what we were talking about: I'm finding that people are coming through the doors of Mecklenburg both interested and confused. They're not skeptics. They're more like very confused mystics. They just need help understanding who this God is and what is He doing with me. And when they experience something, they want to know how to process that experience in relation to this God you're telling me about. And that's helping them see His character, His personality, and His truth through what seems to be silence, distance, mystery.

WS: As I look at the list of books you've written previous to this one, is it fair to conclude that your own writing has experienced the same kind of progression that you say you're seeing in the folks who are coming to your church?

JW: The book that I write at age 42 is different than what I write at 32. And the culture has changed. I think one of my jobs with my calling, with my vocation, is to keep my finger on the pulse of culture. As [Karl] Barth once said, "a newspaper in one hand, a Bible in the other." I do this to know best how to communicate eternal truth to it.

Culture has changed dramatically. When Mecklenburg started, there was more modernity than post-modernity. Now, there's more post-modernity than modernity, though it still intermingles in a bizarre way. I think people's questions about God and spirituality have changed.

But there is a third thing, too. With each successive book, I am more and more having publishers and editors say what I want to say. They're willing to let me do things and say things and not say, "Will you fill this gap in our catalog?" Or, "Can you turn this great sermon series into a book?" When you want to write, and you feel called to write, you take these opportunities and you make the best of them. But they may not be what you stay awake at night thinking about writing, dreaming of writing.

I'm at an interesting place with InterVarsity [Press]. First of all, it's interesting because I've now come full circle. I became a Christian through InterVarsity, and after the success of the previous books, they were willing to say, "Why don't we journey with you? What do you want to write?" And that became the book you now have. They said, "What do you want to write next?" I said a book on culture. The next book will be called "Serious Times." It's Frances Shaeffer's "How Should We Then Live?" meets Gordon MacDonald's "Ordering Your Private World." They said, "Do it." And I know what I want to write after that and after that. Finally, I'm being freed up to do it.

It's interesting that in some of the earlier books I didn't even get to choose the title. I was some two-bit, no-name kid who was supposed to be glad that they were even publishing me. And I was. That was fine. I felt a sense of peace that I was pursuing my craft, my vocation. I'm just delighted that it's reached the stage that I can write more in my own voice, from my own heart. Let more theology come out, more substance and depth.

In terms of Mecklenburg maturing: Of course it's matured as a church. You grow and you mature. But what's been fun for me is that the vision of its maturing has always been there, from day one. You just have realities of church planting. You have a vision of discipleship, but it may take ten years for that to come about. For example, what we're doing now through the Mecklenburg Institute, where we have a quarterly system of community college, where we have 50 classes going on, everything from "Advance Systematic Theology" to "Shepherding Your Child's Heart." If you'd come to our church our first year and critiqued me, you might have said, "It looks like you're doing all evangelism." But, you know what, I'm doing a marathon. I'm not doing a 50-yard dash. Come back in five years. Come back in 10 years. We're building something. This is just a start. So what we're doing now is not so much different from the founding vision as the fulfillment of the founding vision, which was always just be a biblically functioning community.

Strategically, yes, we are known for being a front door for the unchurched. A place where you could bring an unchurched person. Our mid-week service is much more in-depth. But that's just strategy. The vision is a biblically functioning community. How you do it changes all the time.

Editor's Note: A few months after this interview took place, "Embracing the Mysterious God" was nominated for the "Gold Medallion" award by the Christian Booksellers Association, a designation given to the best Christian books of the year. In July 2005, White published "The Prayer That Jesus Longs For." The forthcoming book White mentioned in this interview, "Serious Times," was published in 2004.

Media and the Arts

The World, And All That Dwell Therein

JOEL BELZ

Joel Belz is the CEO of God's World Publishing, the publisher of "God's World News," a weekly, graded news and activity publication for children. "God's World News" is one of the most widely read publications of its kind in the world, particularly popular among homeschoolers and Christian schools. They also publish "World" magazine, which now claims the fourth largest circulation among all newsweeklies – behind only Time, Newsweek, and U.S. News & World Report. The co-author (with Marvin Olasky) of "Whirled Views," Belz is also a weekly columnist for WORLD, and a close observer of the culture and a respected teacher and mentor to many who attempt to apply a biblical worldview to the craft of journalism. At a meeting of the Council for National Policy in suburban Washington, D.C., I spoke with Belz about WORLD Magazine and about how a biblical worldview can and should inform both journalism and the ways we live.

Warren Smith: In one of the presentations we heard today, a speaker said that in 1930, there were only 20 to 30 Christian radio stations in the country, and today there are thousands. Does that sound right to you?

Joel Belz: I don't believe either one of those statistics. I think the record would show that there were more Christian radio station in the early years of broadcasting. And though there are a great number now, I don't think they dominate.

WS: What struck me about those numbers is that even if those are true, they don't say much about the state of the media then and now. Secular radio stations of a half-century ago had more true Christian programming than many so-called Christian stations today.

JB: I'm not sure there is such a thing as a "Christian radio station." Let's put "Christian radio station" in quotation marks. I think there is a profound difference between a "Christian radio station" and a radio station, or a newspaper, run by Christians.

WS: Right. In Scripture, the word "Christian" seems to refer only to people, not things, and particularly not markets. All that said, we do have to identify our market in some way. How do you folks at WORLD preserve a Biblical worldview in your publication without on the one hand losing your focus on your target market or on the other hand becoming a part of the Christian ghetto.

JB: First of all, we have to set aside some of the stories that are of natural interest to Christians. Topics like abortion, gambling, and pornography. Those are the hot button issues for Christians. But there are other issues that Christians should be concerned about. Zoning and taxes and where highways go. So, first of all, we need to change the subjects we're concerned about. We need to spend time on those issues that aren't hot button issues. We need to pick back up on them.

WS: But is there a Christian position on those issues?

JB: I don't pretend to know God's position is on all of these issues, but I do believe that God has an opinion about everything. I go so far as to say that God has opinions on the aesthetics of the neckties you and I are wearing. The reason I say that is that God created color, and if he takes note when a bird falls out of the sky, and the hairs on our heads – which is easy for you and me – then I say he cares about the pattern of colors we use.

Now, does He care about things equally? That is a little iffy, but who am I to sit down here and say, well, God you are not supposed to care about pastels and stripes on a tie. He may surprise me one day. But certainly He cares when poor people get displaced by a superhighway going through their neighborhood. Certainly he

Joel Belz: "I think developing a Christian worldview is logically part of evangelism. It is the far end of the evangelistic process. It is a part of discipleship. It is a part of obedience to Jesus who says to go into all the world and teach people everything I have commanded. You see, we are made in His image. If he hadn't fallen we would see things His way. We would have that 'God's eye view.'"

cares about the justice of taxation and certainly he cares about zoning.

WS: Your life and magazine have been devoted to biblical worldview journalism, sometimes called biblically directing reporting, and to the larger issue of biblical worldview in general. Can you describe in 25 words or less what a biblical worldview is?

JB: I'll say it in fewer words than that. A biblical worldview entails seeking to see things the way God sees them, or as Marvin Olasky sometimes calls it, a "God's eye perspective."

WS: Why is that important? Let me say it another way. Why is it as important as evangelism or other endeavors that Christians spend an enormous amount of resources on.

JB: I think developing a Christian worldview is logically part of evangelism. It is the far end of the evangelistic process. It is a part of discipleship. It is a part of obedience to Jesus who says to go into all the world and teach people everything I have commanded. You see, we are made in His image. If we hadn't fallen we would see things His way. We would have that "God's eye view." But we did fall, so our vision is blurry, and there is a lot of stuff we don't notice, and things we do notice in a warped way, so the development of a Christian worldview is the task of redeeming our perspective on things, so that we once again see things the way He sees them.

Evangelism is the task of helping me see myself accurately. I see myself as a sinner in need of a redeemer, and I see God as the redeemer through Christ. That is the first step, and you go from there.

WS: The evangelical subculture is sometimes called a mile wide and an inch deep. Do you see this lack of a biblical worldview as a reason why we are so shallow, and as a reason why we are having so little impact on the culture?

JB: Absolutely. We reduce the Christian experience to stepping out of Satan's kingdom and stepping into God's kingdom, and that's all there it is to it.

WS: Barrett Mosbacker, whom you know, is fond of saying that biblical principles inform all human pursuits, from theology and philosophy to physics and engineering and math. He sometimes uses the example of building an airplane. It is theoretically and technologically possible to make a passenger airliner that is crash-proof, or at least one in which most crashes are survivable. But the cost would be astronomical. So the engineers who make airliners, and the public who rides in airliners, essentially make moral and ethical decisions about the value of life, and the risk to life, and the cost of these decisions. His point is that having a Biblical world-view is essential even for these kinds of decisions.

JB: I would add, too, that it is important not to make false distinctions. Some people, for example, when it comes to brain surgery they would rather have a totally unbelieving, but excellent, brain surgeon operate on them, rather than a believer who is a bad surgeon. Well, of course. But what I would really rather have is a believing brain surgeon who is very good at his craft, because he sees the person. He sees his patient as an image of God. He sees his hands as accomplishing God's handiwork. He puts that whole package together.

WS: A story you guys did a few years ago that still resonates in the Christian community is the story of the gender-inclusive Bible translation, the so-called "Stealth Bible" controversy. In retrospect, is there anything about that story that you regret, or did you draw any particular lessons from that story?

JB: Well, for one thing, let me say how odd it was, that that story – which was about the Bible – is perhaps still the biggest story in our history. The attention it brought to our magazine is odd because we want to focus on the broader aspects of life.

We said three things in our story. We said there is an effort being made to produce a gender-inclusive edition of the Bible. Second, we said that it was being done in a quiet way. Third, we said that the translation is being culturally driven and not textually driven.

I still think all three of those things are very true, and the more that became known the more true they seemed to be. Was it possible to say what we said in more temperate language? Probably. Do I have regrets about it? That is a very hard question, because in some ways I would have liked to have said it in a little quieter manner. But I am not sure, given the size and resources of the people we were challenging, that we could have stopped what they were doing. We brought it to the attention of the Christian public. That is what were trying to do, I am not sure we could have done it if we were quieter and softer in our approach.

WS: Another story was the McCain coverage. You guys did a story on McCain during the 2000 presidential primary at a time when many evangelicals were trying to make up their minds during the presidential race. Also, William Safire of the "New York Times" editorialized about your coverage, and that increased your notoriety. But the real issue for me, the one I want to ask about, is about the tension you feel as a Christian journalist who is also an active participant in the issues and events you cover. Marvin Olasky, "WORLD's" editor, for example, is actively involved in the "compassionate conservatism" movement. How do you draw a line between being a citizen, a Christian, and a journalist in situations like this?

JB: First, everyone involved in journalism lives in the world, so every journalist has to deal with those things, because every journalist has to deal with the topic of environmentalism. Do you believe in global warming or don't you? Are you an activist about it or aren't you? Do you want your city to be a better city? I don' t know anyone who is neutral on any of those topics.

But we do say that if you are immediately involved in a story, a couple of things have to happen. If you are involved as a decision maker in the story you better withdraw from reporting the story. If you don't withdraw, then certainly your participation should be made very, very clear to the reader. So, in practical terms, in the 2000 primary season, because Marvin Olasky was well known as a supporter of George W. Bush, we asked him not to participate in the reporting on the primary election season, and he stepped aside from that. There was not any surprise to any of our readers that we would be more supportive of George W. Bush than Al Gore, and so we did not feel we had to withdraw from the scene during the general election season.

Let me come back to the Bible issue. I would argue from the get-go I didn't want the publishers of a gender-inclusive Bible to be successful. So we were participants in that battle. But I didn't think in my wildest dreams that we would stop them, so it was a surprise to me that the stories we did actually changed the publishing plans of one of the biggest evangelical publishers in America.

WS: This brings me to my final question. The "Stealth Bible" issue is a great example of Christian journalism making a positive difference. But there are a lot of issues, and not very many journalists pursuing that brand of journalism. Are you optimistic or pessimistic about the future of Christian journalism, or biblically-directed reporting?

JB: Christian radio stations like Salem are now beginning to take the work of news seriously, as well as a host of Christian talk shows. People are now working at it pretty hard.

But, on the other hand, I think we barely scratched the surface because there are so many topics that no one has begun to talk about. Certainly at "WORLD" there are many topics we want to cover more – like healthcare and personal finance, science and technology. Those are all topics Christians need to be thinking about and talking about. We are not doing that well.

On the other hand I take great encouragement because even to scratch the surface reaps rich rewards. I think you felt that way with the "Charlotte World" and some of the stories you've covered. From doing just this little bit you can bring so much benefit. And people are going to discover the riches of living the Christian worldview.

Taking Dominion

MARVIN OLASKY

In Genesis, God tells Adam to "work the land" and "name the animals." No one we know takes these early commandments more seriously than Marvin Olasky. From his home in Austin, TX, Olasky edits WORLD Magazine, the nation's leading Christian news weekly, and the fourth largest news weekly of any kind. He is also a professor of journalism at the University of Texas, and has written several books that have been influential in the training of journalists. His book "The Tragedy of American Compassion" helped define the welfare reform debate of the 1990s, and the ideas in his book, "Compassionate Conservatism," helped define George W. Bush's run for the White House.

Warren Smith: Will the 2000 election be viewed as historic?
Marvin Olasky: There haven't been a lot of elections that have to go past the electoral college process, and this one did just that. The closest comparison in American history is perhaps the 1876 election where the Democratic candidate apparently won 184 electoral votes, but 185 were needed to win. He had apparently taken the states of Florida, South Carolina, and another southern state. But through various chicanery, the Republicans were able to hold on to those states and claim 185 electoral votes,which was the majority needed. There were disputes about which electors were legitimate electors. Congress was divided. The House was a Democratic majority and the Senate a Republican majority. These battles kept going and going and going. In those days the president was inaugurated on March 4. The battles kept going up until the beginning of March.

An agreement was worked out to set up a 15-member board of election commissioners who were supposed to resolve this dispute.

That board decided by a vote of 8-7 that Rutherford B. Hayes, the Republican, should be the next president. The Democrats did not take this lying down at all. This was just a few years after the Civil War, and thoughts of that were still fresh, and there was talk about a new Civil War. There were reports of armed men headed toward Washington. The Democratic and Republican leaders got together and worked out a deal. Hayes became president, but the Democrats got some things they wanted. Since the Democratic base was in the south, Democrats wanted federal troops withdrawn. There were some pork barrel expenditures agreed to. Railroads and other stuff.

WS: So this is not totally unprecedented.

MO: Not exactly once a century. Once every 124 years, let's say. And it worked out peacefully in the end, but in one sense the stakes weren't so high. The federal government was not so big as it is today. It didn't work out so well for blacks in the south. Reconstruction would probably have come to an end anyway. There had been abuses. But the free slaves did need some protection, and they didn't have it any more. So it wasn't a happy deal.

WS: Irrespective of how this election turns out, has there been an erosion of constitutional authority, as some have alleged?

MO: I would say that it is a continuation of the erosion that has taken place over the past eight years. It used to be that dads would hold up their babies and their children at parades as the politicians rode by and would say "There's an honorable person. When you grow up, you can be like that person." We haven't been able to do that for the past eight years, especially for the past couple of years, as Bill Clinton's activities have become more widely known. Whatever president comes in now, there will be about half of the population who may be saying that this is a person who stole the election.

WS: Bill Clinton's approval ratings were high during the impeachment....

Marvin Olasky: "I have a sign up in my office at home that says: "Sensational facts, understated prose." That's what we do 99 percent of the time. Every once in a while there is a time to shout. In chapter 33, I believe, of Ezekiel, it talks about the watchman on the wall. Every once in a while, we find ourselves in that position, when something comes up that is so troubling that we need to shout, that we need to be biblically sensational."

MO: His job performance approval ratings were high. His personal approval ratings were low.

WS: That unusual phenomenon caused some to say that politics has essentially become entertainment. And the role of the media have been to create drama and to generate entertainment value.

MO: Certainly it is the desire of folks in media, both to increase ratings and circulation, and also for their own interests, for things to remain close.

For example, I talk sometimes with Wayne Slater, who is a veteran reporter with the *Dallas Morning News*. He covered Bush's [2000] campaign. Wayne predicted pretty accurately what would happen in the primaries. He said someone would come along and get a lot of attention because reporters want to report. They want a horse race. So we saw that with McCain getting press support.

Then, with both presidential nominations wrapped up in the middle of March, it became a rather boring time for reporters.

In fact, there are a lot of things that factor in to how the media report things. There is ideology, or worldview. Most media are overwhelmingly liberal. We know that. Surveys come out all the time that show that. But they also want it to be close, so sometimes they give a conservative candidate some better play for a while to keep it close. Again, it's partly ratings, but it's partly their own interests. It's just more exciting if it's a close race.

WS: About that time, when it was close between McCain and Bush, WORLD did a major cover story on McCain that generated a great deal of controversy. Without re-hashing that whole episode, I would like to ask if there was anything about your coverage that you repent of?

MO: Basically, it was a good article. Sen. McCain had been getting an easy ride. Things that people needed to know about were not getting reported. I'm glad we did that. In *The American Leadership Tradition* I wrote that we need to know as much as we can about what makes our leaders tick. That includes what kind of husband they are. How they are in their personal relations. The type of stuff we know about local candidates, but often not about national candidates because all we know has been mediated by broadcast structures.

One thing I wish we hadn't done. We went back too far. Some of the things about the break-up of Sen. McCain's first marriage. I tend to have a 10-year statute of limitations, unless older behavior indicates an ongoing pattern of behavior.

WS: How do you make those kinds of decisions? By that I mean this. During that time you were an advisor to George W. Bush and you recused yourself from the editing of that story. Yet, because WORLD Magazine does attempt to report with a biblical worldview, you are not an indifferent spectator to the events you cover. How do you make reporting and editing decisions that do not erode your credibility with your readers?

MO: In that case, I recused myself from editing during the active primary season, where there is real competition. That wasn't so much because there would be conflict in our coverage, but because there were a lot of fine candidates out there. I didn't want our readers to think our coverage was going to be tilted toward one good candidate, when there were still other good candidates in the race.

WS: Keyes and Bauer were still in the race.

MO: Steve Forbes and others, too.

So I didn't see the McCain story until it was in print. Still, I have huge confidence in Nick Eicher and Bob Jones and the other people. They did a terrific job.

But that was a peculiar situation. When the primary season was over, and I got back involved, I think two things were significant. Number one, as a non-profit organization, we were not endorsing any candidate, but anyone who had seen the positions that WORLD has taken over the years, and anyone who knew the positions that Bush was taking, would know that we would be supportive of Bush and we could not be supportive of anyone who thinks it is OK for an abortionist to puncture the skull of a mostly born baby. That is so horrendous that anyone who supports that position loses any right to be president, senator, or anything else. That's such an indication of total depravity.

So that wasn't hard.

At the same time, I had been advising Gov. Bush, especially in the early part of 1999 when he was putting some flesh on the bones of compassionate conservatism, and I really pulled away from that in the last half of the year, and this year I haven't talked with him at all. I have friendly relations with people in the campaign, and every once in a while I shot an e-mail off to them when there was something I just could not resist. But in general I have tried to maintain a distance.

WS: On another story, the so-called "stealth bible" story of a few years ago, the gender-neutral New International Bible story. That story caused a sensation in the Christian community. Were you happy with that story, and with what happened downstream from that story?

MO: I have a sign up in my office at home that says: "Sensational facts, understated prose." That's what we do 99 percent of the time. Every once in a while there is a time to shout. In chapter 33, I believe, of Ezekiel, it talks about the watchman on the wall. Every once in a while, we find ourselves in that position, when something comes up that is so troubling that we need to shout, that we need to be biblically sensational. If you read the Bible, you see lots of examples of sensational writing. In Judges, there is that horrendous situation where the Levites' concubine is gang-raped and killed and cut up in 12 pieces and mailed to the 12 tribes. This is a grisly chapter, but God's inspired writers put it there.

Yes, we know we're not inspired. We're fallen sinners. We're thoroughly limited in our understanding. But one of the very clear things, it seems to me, is "Don't misquote God." It's fine for ministers to exegete a passage; it's fine for commentators to explain it. But it's very important that you don't deliberately set out to take what God's inspired writers wrote and turn it into something that is politically correct and intellectually fashionable. That was our concern.

We had dramatic writing. A dramatic cover. I'm very proud of what we did there. The story itself was in a sense a developing story. We had enough of a story to reveal what was going on. We learned more and there were new developments, so we wrote another story. And then, of course, there were attacks. We responded, explaining what we had done. The one thing that would have been better would have been to have all the information at first. But there are some stories where you have to go with what you've got, and when people see that you're serious about proceeding, then people come forward and tell you more. If you didn't have the first story, you couldn't have gotten the second. It wasn't one perfect story, but overall it was very good, and I'm glad that we are able to awaken the church.

WS: Were you disappointed in how the Christian community responded to that story? It raised issues of authority and accountability that are troubling for the evangelical church.

MO: I was disappointed in how *Christianity Today* and the Evangelical Press Association responded. But overall, I was very impressed with how people responded. Jerry Falwell called me and congratulated us and reprinted thousands of copies of the article. That raised the alarm. Lots of other people. Jim Dobson came forward and wrote a column for us and was instrumental in creating an agreement not to change the NIV. Academic life does not naturally produce profiles in courage, but some in academic life stood up boldly. Vern Poythress of Westminster Seminary. So overall I was very pleased.

WS: These two stories bring up your metaphor of whitewater rapids as a way to describe various kinds of stories. Class I rapids being easy rapids. These are issues that are mentioned specifically in scripture. Class VI being unnavigable. Not only are they not mentioned, but they are very difficult if not impossible to definitively discern a biblical position. And in between are issues that Christians should grapple with, some of which have complex and difficult answers. I've heard you say that homosexuality is Class I because it is specifically mentioned in scripture, but that abortion is Class II. Can you help me understand that distinction?

MO: Abortion is Class II because you have to make one tiny logical step. Number one: Do not kill innocent human life. Number two: the unborn child is innocent human life. Number three: Therefore do not kill unborn children. There is a very small logical step from one to two. You could say that an unborn child is not human life, and many do. On what basis you could say that, especially these days, seems incomprehensible to me. Nonetheless, there is that tiny logical step that you must take. There is no direct prohibition of abortion.

WS: Are there issues that the evangelical church is not treating with the seriousness that they should and, on the other hand, are there issues that we are treating too dogmatically that are in fact more complicated that we like to think they are?

MO: When it comes to the issue "don't misquote God." Yes, there are passages that are difficult to translate. But those passages are not the problem. The problem comes from those passages where we know what it says, we just don't like what it says.

Sometimes, there is a distinction between the principle and the methodology. For example, caring for needy people is Class I. We're told that over and over in the Bible. Exactly the way to carry this out in our society I would call Class III. I believe there very definitely is a biblical position on welfare. But it takes some study. I see a lot of people taking a Class III and turning it into a Class VI. Saying, well, the Bible doesn't have anything to say to us there. To make it harder than it is. A humorist said it wasn't the hard parts of the Bible that troubled him, it was the easy parts.

The Ten Commandments, for example. "Thou shalt not commit adultery." Very, very clear. Very, very hard. Woodrow Wilson was the son of a Presbyterian minister who had an adulterous affair with an unhappy married woman and later said you shouldn't commit adultery unless there is an unhappy woman you can comfort. It's not the unclear stuff we have trouble with. It's the clear stuff that we break and then look to justify.

WS: Another of your areas of study has been the history of American journalism. You have identified the rise of the revivalist preachers in the late 19th century as one of the contributing factors in the decline and increasing secularization of both journalism and of American culture. Many evangelicals consider Charles Finney, for example, a hero.

MO: There was a lot of good that came out of these revivals, but there were also a lot of problems. For example, it became common to think of newspapers as dens of iniquity. Christians should stay away from them. They did. It was as if they were saying "Mommas, don't let your babies grow up to be journalists." Christians gave up in this whole area, with very tragic consequences.

This is just one area. There are other areas. For example, the emphasis of subjectivity and emotions.

WS: There were also issues of theology and eschatology bound up with the revivalists that were extra-biblical. That led to a kind of separatism and resignation.

MO: Yes. There's that. I'm not firmly in any one camp there.

There is a kind of pre-millenialism that in no way harms the idea that Christians should be involved in journalism or other enterprises. But clearly there is a kind of pre-millenialism that teaches that anything we do is the equivalent of re-arranging deck chairs on the Titanic. And all the stuff we do, such as putting out newspapers, doesn't matter. I don't think that's the way God works. I think God calls us to be stewards, to take dominion over the world.

A captain is always supposed to know the condition of his vessel. Christians, in taking dominion, should know the state of the world.

Still Wide-Eyed

NICHOLE NORDEMAN

When Nichole Nordeman's "Wide Eyed" debuted in 1999, it resulted in a Dove nomination for "Best New Artist." Though this album was well-received by the Christian community, it was her second album, "This Mystery" that was in some ways more "wide-eyed" than the first. Fewer simple answers, and more awe at the complexities of life and the Mystery that is God. It resulted in her being named 2000's Female Vocalist of the year by the Gospel Music Association. Since then, her success was continued, with critically acclaimed albums "Woven and Spun" (2002) and "Brave" (2005), both of which produced Top 10 Christian radio lists. This interview took place in 2002.

Warren Smith: What was it like in putting the second album out? There's kind of a mythology around the sophomore jinx, that there's more pressure. Did you feel that?

Nichole Nordeman: Absolutely. I definitely did, and as the old saying goes, you have 20 years to write your first album and eight months to write your second. I did struggle a lot, even on a real practical level, just finding time. I had to record my record sandwiched between two tours. That was really challenging and I'm not sure very conducive to creativity. Then I also struggled with content. I had said everything I needed to say, I thought, that was near and dear to my heart on my first record and so it was kind of like, "Okay, Lord, what's next?" I did a lot of soul-searching and a lot of reading that inspired me, and eventually, like anything, it was fine. It ended up being fine. But, boy, it was a struggle.

WS: Did you end up being happy with the album?

NN: Yes. Very happy with the album. It's certainly a departure. Maybe not a departure, but just a broadening of what the first record was. And the third album will be even more so, so I think it's really representative of where I was musically and spiritually.

WS: And what were you reading? What did you read to get you prepared for the other albums?

NN: I stumbled upon Madeleine L'Engle's *Walking on Water*, which is really a well-kept secret, but it's starting to surface in a lot of artistic circles. Just a brilliant book about faith and art – not just music at all. Just about art in general – sculpting and dancing and painting and how do we honor the Lord through our art and do it authentically and do it excellently. So it was just sort of really what I needed at the time.

A good friend recommended it and it was really interesting and very full circle, and about a year after that L'Engle's publishing house contacted me. They had heard about the influence that her writing had had on my writing, and I was able to do a foreword to a re-publication of her book, so that was a great honor. I have not met her to date, but I would love to. Just a brilliant writer.

WS: What else? Anything else that you were reading during those days?

NN: You know, I am just a complete book junkie, so I probably had three or four things going. That particular book sort of jumped out as one that most influential for sure, but I am constantly reading.

WS: That book and Madeleine L'Engle in general, and of course the title of your album, *This Mystery*, go against the grain of what we see in a lot of evangelicalism these days, which is to say, "I want an easy answer or at least I want an answer." There seems to be a difficulty with a lot of evangelicalism with coming to grips with the reality that the more you know, the less you know. That all you can do is approach mystery-you don't really understand it.

NN: That's right. That's exactly right. Coming from an evangelical background, I did not grow up feeling comfortable with a God

Nichole Nordeman: "Coming from an evangelical background, I did not grow up feeling comfortable with a God of mystery and a God of question marks and a God of who knows? I was much more comfortable, as we all are, with some very easy and, at times, cliché answers. But I really had trouble at a couple points in my life reconciling what I knew to be an easy answer in Sunday school and what I was experiencing in real life, which just didn't just seem to be that easy, as my teachers made it sound to be."

of mystery and a God of question marks and a God of who knows? I was much more comfortable, as we all are, with some very easy and, at times, cliché answers. But I really had trouble at a couple points in my life reconciling what I knew to be an easy answer in Sunday school and what I was experiencing in real life, which just didn't just seem to be that easy, as my teachers made it sound to be. So, like any sort of crisis of faith, I think they call it growing pains for a reason. It is painful, but there is growth, and it's been really important for me to learn how to approach God with the sense of wonder and awe and not a sense of smug "been there, done that" thing that people who have grown from the church have.

WS: Do you find that the industry in general is moving in that direction or not? As the Christian music industry becomes more sophisticated and as the money gets bigger and therefore the stakes get higher, has there been more of a tendency or less of a tendency Christian music to be more formulaic, more sticking to the tried and true, more afraid to take risk? Or is there greater diversity because of that?

NN: Certainly without question there is great diversity. I don't think that I would have gotten a record deal five years ago, or ten years ago maybe. There is a whole lot of room now for a lot of different kinds of expression. Expression that's still really selling is the stuff that we're most familiar and comfortable with, if you're talking about numbers, and I'm totally okay with that. I mean, one of the things that I love about Christian music is that there is kind of something for everybody, and that wasn't the case for me growing up. Once I outgrew loving Sandy Patty and Michael W. Smith, I was pretty bored as an adolescent. There wasn't a whole lot to capture my interest, and so I just turned on pop radio and have been and top 40's fan every since, which isn't a bad thing. But the point is that there really is something for everybody, and if I had an eight-year-old little girl, I would be thrilled to death with some of the Christian music alternatives to Britney Spears, and I would really appreciate that as a mother. If I had a 16-year-old kid, I would appreciate the other stuff, so I'm not critical of that at all, but I am appreciative that because of that there is a place for me to carve out a niche, whereas there really would not have been a while back.

WS: Today, the sales pressure is there at every turn. But your albums are selling all right.

NN: Doing okay.

WS: Do you feel pressure from your record company that they have to perform at a certain level or we're going to have to have a conversation about this?

NN: I think in the back of every artist's mind that pressure exists, and it's not pressure from the label – a label is a business, and the realities of my business are I work for a fantastic label with a bunch of really inspired and committed people to happen to love the Lord. They answer to people in New York who hold stock in the company and may not even know the Lord. That's the reality of business, so if my numbers aren't performing, at some point the reality of that will be a parting of ways. I would never hold anybody responsible for that because that's just how it goes. But, no, I certainly do not feel pressure to outperform the next record. That's always the hope. It's my hope, it's my marketing director's hope, it's my label president's hope. But that's any business. You want to do well, you want to succeed, and I don't know that there's anything wrong with being motivated by success, and certainly by excellence. I think more than anything, I feel a commitment from my label to make excellent music. In fact, I've had several conversations recently with people over there who have said, "Nichole, take your time. We don't want the wrong record. If it's going to take you a little while longer if you just missed deadline A or deadline B, we'd so much rather you make the right record than turn in something just because it's time." I really appreciate that kind of support.

WS: You got a big award last year [Female Vocalist of the Year]. How has that changed your life?

NN: It really hasn't. I know it sounds so cliché, but truly it was a shock, and I was a little bit nervous about "what does this do"? Because I happen to sort of like the pace at which my little ministry is plugging along and selling enough records to keep me happy, and the gigs that I have are relatively small and intimate, like tonight. I like the size of everything right now, and I was a little fearful that winning that award would in some way amplify everything, and it really didn't.

WS: You mean, force people to say we've got to capitalize on this?

NN: Yes. Maybe if I had a record coming out the week after. And I'm sure they will. That title – Female Vocalist of the Year – will certainly show up on many marketing things.

WS: And it won't disappear either. Twenty-five years from now you will still have been the Vocalist of the Year.

NN: Yes, but honestly, day to day it hasn't changed my creative process, it hasn't changed much about my traveling, gigging and touring. More than anything, it was just a really nice and very humbling affirmation from my peers. I'm really honored that somebody thinks this is worth listening to.

WS: Who do you look up to whenever you're in either a spiritual dry spot or creative dry spot, who within the industry do you feel has a lot of wisdom?

NN: Margaret Becker has been a good friend to me, and just short of calling her a mentor, she really has mentored me through some pretty tough decisions and tough spots, and has made plenty of her own career mistakes and would own up to them right here. She's just really honest. I'm so drawn to authentic people, and she is such an authentic person. John Mayes who was in A & R [artist and repertoire] forever and is now starting his own thing. He's the guy who signed me. He remains just a real voice in my life. Darryl Harris, who was chaplain for GMA [Gospel Music Association] for a couple of years and started Star Song, is just another solid, real guy. Those are people that in a very personal way inspire me and have helped.

WS: What is your life like whenever you're making an album, like you are now. Because you're here tonight, you were in Washington, DC, last night. I imagine a lot of your concerts are kind of weekend gigs and then during the week you're working on the album, is that right?

NN: It's different every week, and this is a real time of transition for me because I just moved to Dallas, and I am finding out for the first time that is not nearly as easy as it looked on paper to live in Dallas and make a record in Nashville and still give time and attention to this brand new marriage. Then, to still be creative in the middle of all of those things. It's a real challenge. I definitely won't lie. Creatively, this is a difficult time for different, other reasons than it's been difficult before. Everybody has writer's block, everybody struggles, but even just logistically, how do you work on the weekends and still make money and still be home and be a wife. I don't even have kids! I can't even imagine introducing that into the equation right now. So, it's a challenge. Everybody's learning. My label's learning how to deal with some boundaries I've put up and I'm learning how to try to honor their deadlines with good music. It's just a learning process.

WS: How do you write? Do you close the door and write with a piano or guitar, do you write the lyrics first, or do you just kind of turn on the tape recorder on and start doodling on the piano? What do you do?

NN: Probably the way it happens the most is that I just sit down at the piano – I don't play anything else, just the piano. For whatever reason, for me driving is real therapeutic, not with any particular destination, but just kind of getting on the road and going. I've written entire songs before in the car and then gone home and tried to find melodies and tried to hammer out accompaniment and stuff. That's what I'm learning. You don't always have the luxury of writing the way you want to. There's not always a piano with a couple of candles in a quiet room that you can just sort of slip away to and get inspired. You've got the back of the tour bus and you've got airports, and you've got airplanes. You've got all kinds of places where you just have to be listening for ideas.

WS: When you write and you get a song to a place where you're pretty happy with it, do you then run it by other people that squeeze it down for you a little bit?

NN: Yes. Oh, absolutely. In fact, that's where we are right now. I've chosen a handful of songs that we know are "for sures" on the record and the rest are sort of unwritten, so every time I write something now, the next step is sending it to my producer.

WS: Who's producing this? Is there one guy producing the new one?

NN: Mark Hammond is producing half of it. Charlie Peacock's doing the second half, which I'm totally excited about.

WS: Have you actually been in the studio with Charlie yet?

NN: No, next week is the first time. We've had a lot of talk, but next week is the first actual time together.

WS: He is like the "producer of the millennium," so you want a guy like Charlie Peacock involved in the creative process, right? And yet on the other hand, you must have some ideas about what you want the song to sound like.

NN: I really don't. A lot of people go into the studios with very definite ideas. "Okay, Charlie, here's what I'm thinking on this song." And honestly, for me, I can't get past the song. It is so about the song for me that I don't ever hear, unless it's an obvious thing.

I just don't hear arrangements and I don't hear production, and I'm always so excited and delighted to take a song that's just a rough piano vocal, hand it over to a producer, and hear what they hear at the end – it just blows my mind. Because all I can hear is this little piano thing.

WS: Is that typically the way it is with you? You will go in with pianos and vocals?

NN: That is it. That is the extent of my pre-production. My ear has grown and developed a little bit, and so I'm at least able to hear what I don't like. And that's a lot of it for me. When Mark comes to the table with something-I've given him a piano/vocal, he's taken it in a direction. Sometimes I can't even articulate what it is that I like or don't like about it, but I know when it's not where it needs to be, and I know when he nails it too. It's finding the vocabulary to attach to that that's so hard. I think like a songwriter and not like a producer.

WS: If you could fast forward five, ten years from now and you have a body of work, what message are you crafting, or what do you want the legacy of that body of work to say?

NN: I want the legacy to be something that can be something you'll want to put on in ten or fifteen years. If I never sell one more record than I have on these last two records, I would be fine with that. I really would. And I probably won't sell more than that unless the industry shifts dramatically, and suddenly – like the Sarah McLachlan story where she's been doing her stuff for 15 years and suddenly her stuff got cool. She didn't change a thing about it. If that happens, that would be great. That would just sort of luck of the draw, but that can't be a goal. And there are days when you sort of start to move in that direction. You've had just a few too many business meetings and suddenly you're speaking in stats and that's just not a good place for me to be in, so I have to come back to that very question. What is this really about? It's about making great music. It's about at the end of the day feeling like you've done something excellent that honors God and that hopefully has connected with some other people and that can stand on it's own merit down the road. I would so much rather leave that kind of a legacy than some sort of giant impression flash in the pan, trendy thing.

WS: I know you've only got two albums out, and you've probably got in your head some of the stuff that you're writing now. What have you done so far that, in your opinion, would fit that category? That when you listen to it today, you say, "boy, I really am proud of that. It hasn't been a long time, but at least so far it holds up" and that you think will hold up over time.

NN: I think "Every Season" is probably the best song I've ever written. I don't know if I could ever write a better one. And I say that with as much humility as I can and as much objectivity as I can, but that's the work that I'm most proud of. I can't use that as a barometer, I don't think; I can't hold that up to everything. I don't think I could hit that again. But I felt that same way about some stuff on the first record, too, so I don't know. There's such a delicate balance of raising the bar on yourself all of the time but not beating yourself up if you don't hit it. Sometimes there is just meant to be a moment just once in a lifetime, and that may have been my moment. That may have been the best thing I ever do. If that's the case, then that's fine, but I should keep trying.

Rediscovering Community

MICHAEL CARD

Michael Card has long been one of the most thoughtful voices in Christian music. He was a part of the "first wave" of Christian music in the early 1970s, playing in churches and coffeehouses and releasing critically acclaimed albums. I recently sat down with Michael Card to talk about creativity and the evangelical church.

Warren Smith: In "Scribblings In The Sand," you observe that in the beginning, God created. It is the first character quality we learn about God. But it doesn't seem that the church teaches much about how Christians should imitate God in this way.

Michael Card: When we first meet God, He's an artist. He's not a theological entity on a throne. He's a painter, basically, stepping back and forth from a canvas. It is a shame that the church has overlooked this, because the basic tools that you need for creativity are the tools you need to be a disciple. You need a servant's heart, you need obedience to a call from God, and you need an understanding of biblical humility. So I think creativity is a wonderful way to teach people to be a disciple.

WS: What can and should the church do about this?

MC: Some churches are doing a lot. Other churches are not only not doing a lot, but they're pushing the process back. We just came from a church in Asheville, NC, that had a resident composer on staff. They had a school of music in the church. It was a huge church with lots of money. On the other end, there are still certain churches that say that certain rhythms and chord intervals are demonic. It's almost always a power and control issue. There seems to be an element in the church that is afraid of creativity and they do their best to limit it.

WS: You have spoken of the difference between the corporation and the community in the creative process, in the formation of the Christian artist. You say that what they need is community, but what they get is corporation.

MC: The church is the community, or should be. I trace a lot of what is wrong with contemporary Christian music with the fact that early on the church closed the door on us. I wasn't allowed to play in my own church in the early 70s. What happened is that Christian music took root outside the church. I believe that a lot of the problems we have now is due to that. And in the late 80s, when the church invited us back, they invited us back for the wrong reasons. It was about power and money. Christian music became popular and profitable and the church wanted a piece of this. Those are the wrong reasons, but churches too have become industrial. They have executive pastors, and have corporate structures that nobody seems to be questioning very much.

WS: If you were going to question that structure biblically, what would that questioning sound like?

MC: I think the question would be simply: What is your basis? The basis of any industry is power and money. It's not serving people. The basis of community is letting go of power and money. Unqualified acceptance that is not based on performance. This is the hallmark of community, which is what the church should be. But as the point becomes power and money and more people and a bigger building, then those more delicate aspects of community become trampled.

It seems ironic that in the era of the mega-church the impact of the church is decreasing rather than increasing. That's a symptom that should be stopping people in their tracks. But no one is willing to say that the emperor has no clothes. I look at the gospels and the life of Jesus, and I see no precedent for bigger and better. He poured his life into three men, or the twelve. It's an upside down value system that explains how the Kingdom really works. Upside

Michael Card: "I trace a lot of what is wrong with contemporary Christian music with the fact that early on the church closed the door on us. I wasn't allowed to play in my own church in the early 70s. What happened is that Christian music took root outside the church. I believe that a lot of the problems we have now is due to that. And in the late 80s, when the church invited us back, they invited us back for the wrong reasons. It was about power and money. Christian music became popular and profitable and the church wanted a piece of this."

down by the modern world's reckoning. Saints who are imprisoned in obscure parts of the world are forwarding the Kingdom of God far more than big TV preachers with huge budgets. The Kingdom doesn't grow by observation. It grows like a seed. It's a mystery. The growth is often hidden. It's relational. It's one at a time and it costs. American Christianity has evangelism the other way around. We have impersonalized evangelism. We do evangelism by getting people to put their names on a card. A professional does the work.

WS: This sort of critique of the church is powerful, but it has also cost you. Do you think it takes courage to talk to the evangelical church in this way?

MC: I don't think of myself as a courageous person. I've had my courage tested on a few occasions and I've failed fairly miserably. No, either something is true or it is not true. Untruth has become popular and gives you more power. That's still no reason to embrace it. At least to question it. I just don't see people questioning it. Not even young people. Young people are supposed to be questioning this, not me! Not old guys like me. When I was in college, that's what we were going. Why are we doing things this way? We should be asking this: Why is worship an industry? Why is Time-Life selling worship collections on TV? Something that is as intimate to the church as worship has become an industry. Some see this as a wonderful triumph for the church.

WS: But you don't?

MC: No, not at all. The gospel doesn't pay, the gospel costs. At the point that getting paid becomes the issue, that's a problem. And we aren't even asking these questions.

WS: You talked about Jesus pouring his life into the twelve, and into the three – Peter, James, and John. You've written a book about Peter. Why Peter?

MC: Peter really chose me. I was working through Acts, and I kept encountering this person I thought I knew but I discovered I didn't know at all. I wonder if this hasn't given me some of what we were just talking about. Because the interesting thing about Peter is that he lets go of power. If anyone was in position to become the leader, the head guy of the church, which he really was for a while as the leader of the Jerusalem church when the Jerusalem church the main church, it was Peter.

But Peter, in order to reach out to the Gentiles, to be obedient, which we see in the whole Cornelius affair, Peter lets go of his leadership of the church in Jerusalem and becomes a missionary. James becomes the head of the Jerusalem church. Even in later life, even though Peter has this unique title given to him by Jesus, "the rock," Peter encourages us to become "living stones." Peter routinely let go. I think that's what we're called to do. Jesus let go of his authority, he let go of power. John the Baptist said "I must become less important and he must become more important." I see that in Peter's life. Eugene Peterson, in his introduction to First Peter, talks about what a refreshing thing that is to see in the church today, where so few church leaders think about letting go of power. The treadmill of people in ministry looks like this: "power is good, and the more power I have the more my ministry will expand, therefore I will go for more power."

And I'm on it too. Every day I have choices. Do I do something that is in a gray area that will give me a wider audience? A wider audience is good. More record sales. That's good. I have to make those choices all the time.

WS: How do you make those choices? What principles should guide that decision making process?

MC: It is hard. In this culture, to maintain purity is difficult. Even if you think that Time-Life selling worship is bad, you might look in your wallet and discover that you have a credit card from the same company that owns Time-Life. Or if you think it's OK and then you discover that there's a pornography business owned by

Time-Life.

Community has a lot to do with the way we should make those answers. Again, we come back to community. The guy who mentored me talked about developing a lifestyle of listening. This idea of listening to the Word, listening to your own life, listening in prayer. For me, it's all about community. When big decisions come up, there is a group of people who I go to and say, "What do you think about this?" I think that's the biblical approach. One of the most deliberate things Jesus did was to develop community. The church is community. We're not supposed to do these things in isolation.

WS: Some of the decisions that have been made by the Christian music industry have been motivated by artists who have fallen into moral failure and the industry had to decide whether to act like community or corporation.

MC: That's a great point. Here's my position on this. When those events happen, I can remember a time when I was morally outraged, too. But now I've come to realize this: Why should the industry care about morality? They care only insofar as it gives them more money or more power. I'm no longer disappointed or surprised than an industry, even a Christian industry, doesn't especially care about moral accountability. That's a community value. Why should the industry care? They care only insofar for a while there is a dip in record sales. And sometimes there's a spike in record sales. The truth is that that's not their job. They've said they're an industry. They are an industry. Exercising accountability is not their burden anymore. Why should they care? And why should I get outraged when they don't care? That's just simple logic.

WS: Well, yes, but aren't we supposed to care?

MC: Yes, but my point is that an industry is incapable of caring for your soul. The industry reduces church members to consumers. That's all they are to the industry. That's not to say that within the industry there aren't people who are Christians. There are wonderful, godly people who are executives in record companies. There are godly artists. So it's never as simple as we want it to be.

WS: Who are you listening to now? Who are some of those godly artists doing great work today?

MC: Michael McDonald. He's a wonderful example of someone who stayed in secular music but has been a wonderful light. He is doing confessionally Christian music now, but he is staying in a secular context. I have huge admiration for him and I listen to his music an awful lot. Kirk Whalum, a jazz saxophone guy. He's a wonderful Christian man who was once challenged by his church to quit playing jazz because it's the world's music. But he realized he was called to stay in that world. I know Kirk well. I don't know Michael McDonald at all.

WS: At the risk of asking a nonsensical question, let me ask this: are there pockets of community in the industry? If so, where are they?

MC: It's a fair question, and that's the reality. There are pockets of community in the industrial American church, right? Even in these huge mega-churches there'll be little pockets of community. Within the music business, there are pockets. I meet with a group of guys. Phil Keaggy, Steve Green, Kirk Whalum, and some players whose names you may not recognize but who are great artists. We read books together, we stay in touch, pray together when we can. It's not formal or programmatic. But more important than that is for the artists to be involved in community outside the industry. We tried to build a thing called Covenant Artists Communities, but after beating my head against the wall for five years I realized that wasn't going to work. That's not what artists need. Artists need to be in community with all sorts of people. With people who work at the Saturn plant, and pastors, people who do all different things.

WS: One of the things communities do is raise children. You have four children. How do you communicate these ideas about community and art and creativity to children?

MC: I think the most powerful way is when my children see me spending time with other men that I walk closely with. When I'm on the road and my water heater goes out, there are a half-dozen men my wife can call who at 2 in the morning would be happy, not just feel obligated, to come. They'd be happy to be asked. Those sort of real, lived-out, incarnate expressions of community make the difference. I talk about it all the time, but seeing it is more important.

WS: How much are you on the road these days? And given the fact that you've been so critical of the industry, how has that affected your own economic well-being?

MC: I do about 80 shows a year. And all of the talk about industry vs. community and all of that, I would say that up until a couple of years ago, I didn't notice that it really hurt me. That is, until about four or five years ago. The result of it is that I have just had to work a lot harder. Without a record company to pay for the production of records, it's harder. I sometimes wonder why it has to be so hard. But then I just listen to what I say to other people, about the cost of discipleship. I'm never going to retire. I mean, who retires from ministry? But I am 46, and I had hoped that at some point I could gradually start slowing down, but I work more now than I did ten years ago. I write a book a year, and do a record a year. And we do 80 concerts a year. Now, compared to the price a lot of people pay all over the world, where people are being crucified for their faith in Sudan right now. So working a bit extra is a small price.

WS: You're now writing books, but what books had an impact on you?

MC: Historically, "The Cost of Discipleship" was the big earthquake for me. Dietrich Bonhoeffer. I read it in college, and nothing was ever the same for me. In fact, even the discussion that we just had is just me trying to delineate or clarify what I read in that book. "When Jesus calls a man he bids him come and die." That's powerful enough to have said, but then Bonhoeffer died.

Then came Brendan Manning's "Lion and Lamb: The Relentless Tenderness of Jesus," which is a book about healing our image of God. I think it was at that point that I learned that our emotional life is supposed to be integrated into our spiritual life. I never understood that. I named my son after Brendan Manning, that's how big that book was for me.

Recently, Larry Crabb's new book, "The Pressure's Off: A New Way To Live," even though I don't like the title. He wanted to call it "The Immanuel Agenda," which I think is a much cooler title. That book is going to be a big book for me. It talks about how we use God to get what we want. We say, "I going to do these things and I'm going to include God in the equation and that's how I'm going to get what we want." That's how we all think. That's American Christianity in a nutshell. This book exposes that. He does a brilliant job of articulating that.

WS: When you're at home, are you writing, practicing, planning your next project?

MC: My life, when I'm at home, is that I'm basically a groundskeeper. We have a little family farm. I live in Franklin, Tennessee. We had storms go through recently and I spent last week sawing up trees that had been blown down, and when I get back home I'll split them. I have a little Bobcat bulldozer that I clear trails with, and we're building a retreat center where I live. So I do stuff like that. Four kids, seventeen chickens, five dogs, a horse and a pony.

Which reminds me. Wendell Berry is another big writer for me.

And this whole idea of the Southern Agrarian lifestyle is huge for me. Obviously we can't have a self-sufficient farm. It costs us more to grow vegetables than it would to go to the grocery story and buy them. The chickens, we may break even. But the values of that lifestyle are important to me. I know that it's a bit of a yuppie thing to do, to be out there with my diesel bulldozer. It's not pure Agrarianism. It's sort of a counterfeit, but it's what I do.

The Center Of The Human Heart

ROBERT WHITLOW

Robert Whitlow was a successful attorney with a big law firm in Atlanta who never had any aspirations to be a writer – when suddenly, several years ago, a story came into his head. It was his wife who insisted he write the book, which ultimately became his first novel, "The List." His second novel, "The Trial," won a "Christy Award" for excellence in Christian publishing. Other books followed, and total sales of his novels are now in the hundreds of thousands. Now living in Charlotte, he has been instrumental in forming a non-profit organization dedicated to helping Christians resolve their conflicts outside the court system. And he recently formed a film production company to bring "The List" to the big screen.

Warren Smith: Your books have been described as a Christian version of John Grisham's books. How do you feel about that comparison, and do you feel it's valid or accurate?

Robert Whitlow: I am perfectly comfortable with the comparison. I didn't pattern my try writing after anybody in particular, but there are a lot of similarities in background between myself and Grisham. We are both attorneys and we are both from small southern towns. We came out of a similar cultural background and those common influences have probably in some way created some similarities in our writing.

WS: Interestingly, Grisham claims to be a Christian as well. Yet we don't think of him as a Christian novelist. You have, however, published your books with a Christian publisher. You recently received an award from a Christian organization that honored Christian novels. Is the label "Christian novelist" a false distinction? How do you feel about being labeled a Christian novelist as opposed to a novelist who happens to be Christian?

RW: I like what C.S Lewis said about it. He said that the world does not need more Christian writers; it needs more writers who are Christians. So my desire is to create a work that is as excellent as possible, yet at the same time incorporate into the story the spiritual realities that we believe exist because we are Christians.

WS: There is a tradition of Christian mystery writers. Eliot's plays, or Dorothy Sayres, or even some of Lewis's novels are essentially mysteries or suspense novels. Is it a natural that the suspense or mystery genre lends itself to talking about Christian ideas?

RW: I think that Christian ideas can be communicated in every style of story, in every kind of writing. I kind chose to go the suspense route and my purpose is that I want to create a plot that has sufficient interest to hold readers' attention, whether they are Christians or not. Then, in the lives of the characters, the spiritual aspects surfaces part of the context of the story.

WS: The suspense form is a form that is heavily dependent upon plot. Some would say more dependent upon plot than characters.

RW: People say that, but I really make an effort to have characters with some substance. A little quirky. Things about them that will hold the readers' interest.

WS: Do you think that is one of the reasons your book was singled out for excellence by the Christy Awards judges?

RW: Yes. One of the reviews – I think it was in Publishers Weekly – characterized the development of the characters as one of the outstanding aspects of the book and I think that was one of the things the Christy judges were looking for, in order to try to encourage writers to produce things that don't have flat stereotypical characters.

WS: Is that what is wrong with a lot of Christian fiction these days? Are Christian writers so focused on trying to make a spiritual point that they don't get into the heart of the character?

RW: Yes. I think that is accurate, and I think that has been one of the criticisms that has been leveled against inspirational or Christian fiction. It was preachy and sentimental and it failed to rise to the level of technical quality that was in the secular marketplace.

WS: Of course, those characteristics are hard even for the experienced writer. You seem to have hit a stride in your writing career after only two novels – unless you've been writing for years and not telling anyone about it.

RW: No. This is the only fiction I have ever written. I started "The List" in 1996.

WS: But surely you had an interest in fiction?

RW: No, I had no ambitions. No desire to see my name on the cover of a book. Everything I had written previous to this involved teaching materials that I use myself. Historical articles. I am very interested in revival -- revivals of the past, the Welch revivals, the revivals in Scotland and England. And the personalities that were involved. I was just a lawyer and I got the idea for "The List" in 1996 and was a complete and total novice, but talked to my wife and she said you need to write this and so that is where is started.

WS: What gave you the idea for "The List"?

RW: I had thought about the spiritual dynamic that I had seen worked out in so many people's lives. The way they are influenced by the past generations of their families – both for good and for bad. Some people can trace their own spiritual pilgrimage and they give credit to a grandmother who prayed for them. So there is a positive side to that as well as a negative. But you have heard of so many people that have a problem with alcohol and their father had a problem with alcohol.

So I thought it would be interesting to trace the generational

Robert Whitlow: "When I talk about revival, my desires and expectations are beyond just a series of evangelistic meetings. I am in favor of that, but I am interested in something that has an impact on the society. In the old days the revival would come and the bars would close and the jails would empty and the people would spend their time loving God and one another. That is my interest in revival."

influences back to the time of the Civil War for a particular family and show how the good and evil played out in the life of a contemporary character. Good and evil is the greatest theme that exists in literature, because that is the ultimate struggle in the universe.

But the story begins without any clue about those dynamics. I came up with the idea of the secret society that started back in the Civil War time that had the appearance of something good, but had a seed of evil within, because of the greed of the people and their decision to trust money as their security instead of God.

WS: From a marketing point of view, the book tapped into a strain in the Christian community that almost wants to believe that this kind of list exists. Was that going through your mind?

RW: Those particular things were not. I was aware of that, but what I was going after was something that was plausible. In fact, after I started writing "The List" I learned that toward the end of the Civil War Jefferson Davis came through Mecklenburg County [N.C.] with the Confederate treasury, and their desire was to try to get it overseas to continue the fight. Of course, you know the gold didn't make it out of Mecklenburg. There are myths about what has happened to it. But it is likely that Confederate soldiers just took the money as back pay. But none of that inspired the idea behind the story. I was just trying to write something that was plausible, but had an element of drama and a heightened sense of reality.

WS: You mentioned your interest in revival, and obviously you have had a bit of a turn in your own life – from lawyer to novelist, but not all the way to evangelist. What is the relationship between revival and culture?

RW: Well, I do speak on revival, to the extent that God gives me opportunities. But when I talk about revival, my desires and expectations are beyond just a series of evangelistic meetings. I am in favor of that, but I am interested in something that has an impact on the society. In the old days the revival would come and the bars would close and the jails would empty and the people would spend their time loving God and one another. That is my interest in revival.

One of the things that has become my real passion in the books is to portray characters who will encourage people to have a real dynamic life of prayer and to believe there is a reality in that kind of interaction with God. I have a pretty simple theology. I believe God is real and that he is not a cosmic clock maker. He wants to be dynamically involved in our lives on a day to day basis, and that is what I portray in the stories.

WS: The characters that are less spiritually mature in your books behave like pagans might behave. Do you feel any self censorship, or the possibility that a Christian publisher might not have wanted to publish your book if you were more direct in the way you portrayed the non-Christian characters in your book. In other words, are there limitations writing for the Christian genre or Christian audience or did you feel all the freedom that you needed did you do all the things you wanted to do in that regard?

RW: I am glad you asked that question, because that is something I thought about a bit, because I toyed with the idea on the first book of not even writing it for the Christian fiction market. But it became apparent to me quickly that that's who I am and to the extent I can communicate something real it needs to come out of who I am and what I believe.

As far as portraying characters in their lost condition, I will do that, but I will not use some of the graphic language or explicit language or graphic detail of sin that other books would. Of course, most of those things take place in secret in real life. There was a greater expression of art, in my opinion, before we had these graphic depictions of sex and violence. There was more subtlety.

Also, I believe there is a place I can go and other Christian writers can go that nobody else can go because we have a understanding of a kingdom of God and the ways of the spirit of God in the lives of people.

WS: Has there been anything surprising about the reception that you have gotten from either the Christian or secular community?

RW: I don't really have a reference for that. I was writing "The List" for two years and I didn't know that it was going to be published. I wrote it for my wife. I wrote that book to bring her pleasure. I just said, "Lord, I believe you want me to do this and I am going to do it."

WS: Someone once told me that you should write not for an "audience" but for a single reader.

RW: That probably helped me with that book. And then I also enter into a relationship with my characters. They become real to me. I don't write from a detailed outline. I am what an editor told me was an "organic writer." An organic writer creates a scene and introduces characters, not fully knowing what they are going to say or do, and then just allow that scene to develop.

Sometimes I have an idea about where things are going and sometimes I don't, but I really enter into an emotional relationship with the characters. In the first book there are two women who are strong prayers. One is the landlady for the main character, and the other is a lady that helped raised him. I remember one day writing a scene where one of them was engaged in prayer for this main character and I just turned off my computer and got up and said, "God, I realize that these are made up characters, but I want to be like this myself, to have that kind of relationship with you that I can pray with this kind of specificity and be on point with what your will is with this person."

WS: How do you feel you have grown as a writer from the first book?

RW: My technique is better.

WS: Did you learn that in the writing process or did your editor help you with that?

RW: I learned it in the writing process. And I got this book called "Self Editing For Fiction Writers" and that book changed my life because things I knew intuitively I now know cognitively. I was able to apply that in the writing process.

WS: What else inspired your writing?

RW: Well, the greatest influences on modern writing are Ernest Hemingway and the television. Hemingway wrote from a journalistic perspective. Ever since he came on the scene that has been a general trend. Show, don't tell. And, of course, that is what television does.

WS: So as a southern man you didn't read Faulkner?

RW: Yes, I did read Faulkner, and other famous writers, but I can't say any of them had a great influence on my writing. What had more of an impact was visiting my relatives and wanting to hear my uncles tell stories.

WS: Since you have an interest in revival, I understand there was a major revival that took place in this part of the country in the 1800s.

RW: Most of the things that happened around 1800-1805 I kind of associate with the Cane Ridge Revival in Kentucky.

WS: We are now celebrating the 200 year anniversary of these events. Do you think that kind of revival could happen again here?

RW: Yes. I have asked the Lord for that. I would like to participate in some way in a genuine visitation like that in my lifetime.

WS: What's next for you? Are you working on another novel?

RW: I am almost finished with the third book. It's about prayer in the school and the violence of the school issue. It's set in North Carolina in a fictitious town outside of Charlotte. You can have metal detectors – there is wisdom in taking those steps. But as a Christian I believe the greatest response we can have is prayer, because the dividing line between good and evil is in the center of the human heart. That is what the book is about.

Editor's Note: Whitlow finished that third novel, "The Sacrifice," and by 2005 had seven books in print.

Perhaps You Can Go Home Again

Lauren Winner

Lauren Winner's "Girl Meets God" received popular and critical acclaim when it was published in 2000. A native of Asheville, from a locally prominent family, (both her dad and her aunt served in the North Carolina Senate), the story of her life reads a bit like the novels of another famous Asheville native, Thomas Wolfe. Winner, raised by a Jewish dad and a Southern Baptist mom, left the South for New York's Columbia University at age 16. While there, she converted to Orthodox Judaism, but that was just the next step in her spiritual pilgrimage. Upon graduation from Columbia, she studied at Cambridge, where she then converted to Christianity. Her books embrace a thoroughly orthodox Christian theology that attempt to recover the heritage and some of the traditions of Judaism. Her second book, "Mudhouse Sabbath," examines how Jewish traditions can help Christians gain a more biblical understanding of some of life's important rites of passage.

Warren Smith: When you wrote "Mudhouse Sabbath" you included a chapter on weddings without having been married and a chapter on death and mourning without ever having lost anyone close to you. Since then, your mom has died and you've gotten married. Do you want to re-write those chapters now?

Lauren Winner: Do I want to recant? No, if anything, I would add some exclamation marks.

I could go on at length about mourning. It's been interesting to me that the mourning chapter has been the chapter that most Christian readers said was the one that struck them. And it has been only two months and change since my mother died, but now I would add an "amen, sister" to the end of that chapter. In many ways, the church has been wonderful and supportive during my mother's illness and her death. People really did show up intensely for about two weeks. But those were two weeks that I felt fine. I was so exhausted from her illness, and in a fog. Now, six to eight weeks after her death, it's really started to hit. I've been having a lot of very disturbing dreams about her illness. I think that if I called a friend and said I'm really despondent I'm sure my friend would talk with me about it but there isn't a choreographed way in the church for either the mourner to walk through that or for the community to participate in communal bereavement. So I think because of my own experience and because the chord it seems to have struck with so many readers I do really think this is an area where the church and where secular society needs to do some work.

On the wedding front, I would make a very similar point, which is that there needs to be more of a role for the community. I think my particular community was particularly involved in the making of Griff's and my marriage. I hope they will continue to be involved in the sustaining of it. But already, only six weeks into being married, it is already clear to me that this really is a communal project. And Christians have absorbed the American modern idea that marriage is private. And that even Christians who really strive for transparency with one another, and accountability, when it comes to their marriage they may not be willing to be so transparent. And it's hard, of course. You don't want to talk about these things. What are the three big things they tell you you'll fight about? Sex, family, and money. Who wants to talk about these things, even with fairly close friends? But I'm daily more convinced that this is necessary. And, frankly, we know that Christians in America have as high a divorce rate as non-Christians, which to me is the single most depressing statistic about failures in the church. But I think that if we were more intentional about recognizing that marriage is a community project, we might be able to get those numbers to turn around.

WS: Your own transparency, especially about sex, has been one of the more controversial aspects of your own writing. An article that you did for beliefnet.com, in particular, got a lot of comments. When that happened, especially when the reactions from the Christian world started, was that a surreal experience for you, or was it what you expected?

LW: Part of me expected it, and a part of me was quite taken aback. And the book that I am working on now, which will hopefully be published in a year or so, is a book about chastity.

WS: I'm assuming you're for it.

LW: I am for it! I am absolutely for the orthodox Christian teaching on chastity, but what I am not for is the culture of euphemism that Christians gravitate toward when it comes to sex. I got married when I was 27. I didn't become a Christian until the end of college. I had had sex before becoming a Christian. It's just tough. If you get married when you're 19, it's not as much of a challenge to remain chaste prior to marriage. And the point of saying that – the point of saying that it's difficult and people are failing at it, we know people are failing at it – the point of that is not to throw the traditional teaching out the window. Rather, it's to say that if we as a community spoke more straightforwardly about the challenges in people's lives, we might pastorally be able to support people better in their efforts to live chastely.

I think for me, personally, when I first became a Christian, I knew that Christians weren't supposed to have pre-marital sex. Paul said so. That was the sum total of what I could have said about the subject. On the one hand, that's enough. Paul's very clear. But on the other hand, there is a much deeper reality that Paul is referring to when he says that. I'm interesting in beginning the biblical conversation about this as it starts in Genesis. You really don't have a

Lauren Winner: "The people who are really influencing me on these subjects are Hauerwas, who brings us back to this notion of marriage and community. They're all bound up. I don't see how you can separate an ethic of sex, or premarital chastity, from the community and from marriage. And Wendell Berry, actually, has been someone who has been helpful to me. Because sex is the thing we have most privatized. It really is a community issue."

biblical understanding of marriage and what sex is for and of the created order, then it just sounds like Paul is a mean-spirited killjoy, when in fact Paul is trying to restore the goodness of creation. That's why I think we need to have a more honest conversation in the church.

The people who are really influencing me on these subjects are [Stanley] Hauerwas, who brings us back to this notion of marriage and community. They're all bound up. I don't see how you can separate an ethic of sex, or premarital chastity, from the community and from marriage. And Wendell Berry, actually, has been someone who has been helpful to me. Because sex is the thing we have most privatized. It really is a community issue. One of the things I'm striving to do in this book is to explain why it is a community topic. Why is it anyone's business what anyone – married or not – is doing in their bedroom. The idea that sex is private, and as long as you have two consenting adults it's no one else's concern – I think that's the fundamental lie that secular society tells about sex. The church, to a large degree, has unconsciously absorbed some of that. I've found Hauerwas and Berry both to be very helpful in pointing me to the communal nature of sex.

WS: Stanley Hauerwas is consciously, intentionally Christian. Wendell Berry is Christian in many ways in his worldview, but he does not affirm Christianity intentionally. Consciously.

LW: I find his early essays, particularly "The Body and the Land," helpful. I do not know about his personal piety. He writes very robustly about reality. For me, that's enough.

WS: Did you shop "Girl Meets God" with Christian publishers?

LW: No. I intentionally wanted to publish "Girl Meets God" with a non-Christian press. And part of that was the hope that it wouldn't be ghettoized with the religion books. That it would be taken as a literary memoir. That's happened, some. It would not have been reviewed by the "New York Times" if it had been published by a

CBA [Christian Booksellers Association] press. The other reason is that spiritual memoirs as a genre has been seeing success, people like Kathleen Morris and Anne Lamott, people who have pioneered the contemporary expression of spiritual memoir. The reason spiritual memoir is a great tool for reaching the unchurched, whether you want to call them pre-Christians or seekers or whatever the term would be. There is absolutely a place for "Mere Christianity," for C.S. Lewis and the classic apologetics. And spiritual memoir is not a substitute for that, but there's a whole group of people – and I don't know if this is just a post-modern moment, or if it is partly a generational thing – who are never going to pick up "Mere Christianity," or if they did pick it up they would be left cold by its highly rationalistic, analytical approach. Some of those people might be moved to pick up and then be moved by [a book in which] someone says, "This is my story, of what God did in my life. I'm not, per se, going to tell you what to do with it. You can take it or leave it."

And, in fact, several memoirs like that were influential in my own several years drawn out conversion.

WS: Can you name one or two?

LW: Most influential in this was Frederica Mathewes-Greene's book "Facing East." Which is ironic, because of course I became an Anglican and her book is about her conversion from Episcopalianism to Eastern Orthodoxy. But that book is much more fundamentally about the Gospel. And that book was published by Harper SanFrancisco. I don't know that I would have ever found that book if it had been published by a CBA press. I wasn't at that time in my life frequenting Christian bookstores. So I was happy to be with a non-Christian press because my editor was a fiercely secular Jew. If I could convince my editor, who didn't know the difference between a fundamentalist and an evangelical, I knew I could potentially reach someone like her who might pick the book up in a bookstore. I have also had fantasies about publishing with Algonquin. But I'm thrilled now that the paperback is coming out on a CBA press, because it can get into those marketing channels.

WS: Algonquin has become a storied publishing house in a relatively short period of time, especially as it relates to Southern literature. The trajectory of your life is not unlike some of Faulkner's or Wolfe's characters, itself. You're from Asheville, you go to New York, to Columbia. You end up at Cambridge, and now you're back in the South with a lot of miles and a couple of books behind you. Many of the Fugitive-Agrarians took a similar path. Though none were Jews, to my knowledge, some of them did convert to Christianity along the way.

LW: Well, that's interesting. I am sympathetic to many though not all of the impulses you find in "I'll Take My Stand." I haven't figured out how to extract the racism and do much with the edifice. I don't know that you can. But I was born in 1976. The South that I have grown up in has been very much the New, New, New South. It's a South in which John Shelton Reed is paid by Quaker to be their grits consultant. It's a South in which the real South and the commodified South are absolutely inextricably linked. To some extent that's been true since the 19th century. But I think it is more true than it has ever been. To go back to John Reed. He has this wonderful essay in which he says the only way to figure out where the real South is to look in the Yellow Pages and find out which towns have "Southern This" or "Dixie That" in the titles of the businesses.

Now, it is very different teaching at UVA than being at Columbia. I just finished teaching "Religion in the American South" to a class of 20 students, half of whom are pastor's kids, and many are in the PCA [Presbyterian Church in America]. It's different. Religion in the South is still different from religion elsewhere. On the other hand, the claim that we are a continuation of medieval church is fairly well romanticized. Fundamentalism, after all, is just as much a modernist project as liberalism.

WS: When Andrew Lytle and others said that, I expect they were referring to high-church Anglicanism, and its transplantation to America intact.

LW: Right. But the Episcopal Church in Virginia is not high church. And even if it were, that's not southern religion. Even in those southern pockets where you do have a more Anglo-Catholic, or more Oxford Movement type of church. I mean, please, southern religion is the Baptist church, the Methodist church, the Presbyterian church.

WS: So Flannery O'Connor truly was an anomaly.

LW: Sure, and she knew that. She was very articulate about the particular resources that Catholicism gave her. She didn't say Christianity gave her these resources. Her characters were always protestants. Paul Elie's new book, "The Life You Save May Be Your Own," is a four-part biography of Day, Merton, Percy, and O'Connor. I don't know a lot about Walker Percy, and it was interesting to read this book that is about a great moment in American Catholicism and two of the people are these Deep South writers. In some ways they're not representative of American Catholicism and in some ways not representative of Southern Christendom. That's why it's always hysterical to me when people invoke that "Christ-haunted landscape" phrase of O'Connor's, because I think she meant something different than what those who appropriate the expression.

WS: You have this literary/intellectual life, and yet your family is pretty well-known in North Carolina for their social and political involvement. Your dad is a judge and former state senator. Your aunt was a state senator. Your sister is a pretty well-known lobbyist at the state level. Your mom was well known as a volunteer, sort of a matron of Asheville society. It must seem a bit surreal coming back to North Carolina.

LW: Yes, she was. She was Buncombe County Woman of the Year. The whole Junior League thing. I've spent my life being Dennis Winner's daughter, or Linda Winner's daughter, or Leslie Winner's niece. Now, I get "Are you related to LeAnne Winner?" That's my sister, who I look a lot like, and who is a lobbyist for the school board association. But recently someone came up to my father and said to him, "Are you related to Lauren Winner?" I was thrilled. But his response was, "Why do you want to know?" He wasn't sure if he should claim me!

I guess that in many ways if you looked at me and my parents' life, you would see a lot of disjunctures. My vocational life is in a different field than my parents. My religious commitments are different from theirs. My sister and I are radically different in interests, and tastes, and temperament. The one thing my parents successfully inculcated in both me and LeAnne is a strong feeling for civic participation and public duty. That's not manifesting in my professional life in the same as it is in my sister's, but it's there, and it's something I appreciate in my parents and in my aunt.

I hope someday to come back to North Carolina. My aunt Leslie owns a small piece of property, with some friends, in Ashe County. Even though she has lived in Charlotte for ages, she says that this is what being from Western North Carolina does to you. It calls you. She said, "I just have to own a small piece of it." Western North Carolina inspires in its people a kind of loyalty that is not inspired, I expect, by the Triad. There's a particularity of place, not an arbitrary marketing designation. I remember combing through some things at my mom's house and I came across a clipping from the newspaper when my father first became a district court judge, when he was 28 years old. And they quoted him as saying that when his father opened Winner's Department Store in Asheville the people of Western North Carolina made it possible for my fami-